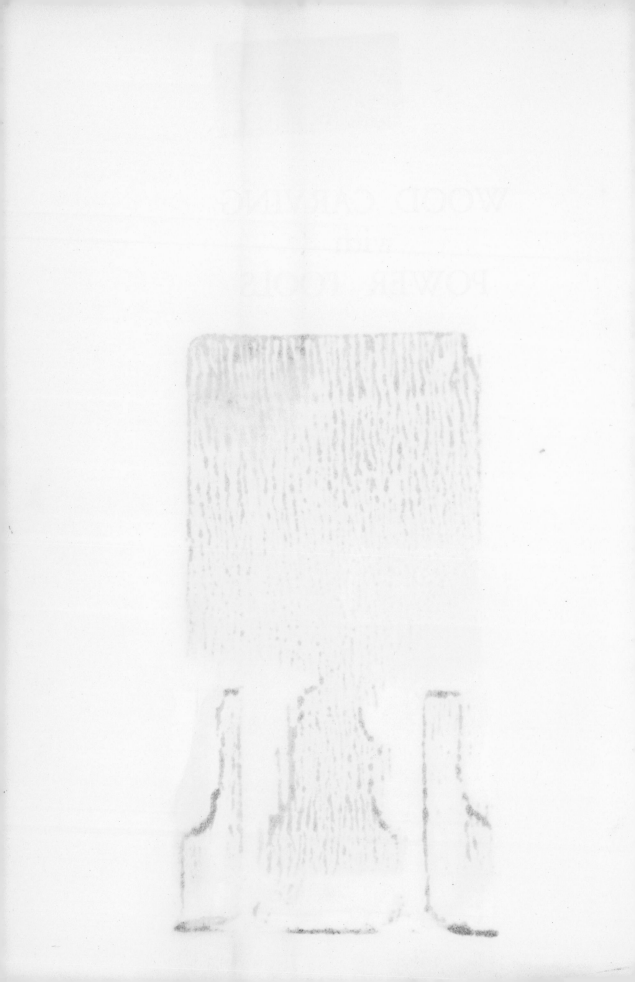

WOOD CARVING
with
POWER TOOLS

WOOD CARVING
WITH
POWER TOOLS

RALPH E. BYERS

CHILTON BOOKS
A Division of Chilton Company; Publishers
Philadelphia - - - - - - - - - - *New York*

Published in Philadelphia by Chilton Company,
and simultaneously in Toronto, Canada, by Ambassador Books, Ltd.

Library of Congress Catalog Card Number 59–9016

Manufactured in the United States of America
by Quinn & Boden Company, Inc., Rahway, N. J.

For
MARY BYERS

Contents

WOOD CARVING
with
POWER TOOLS

Introduction

This book is for the man who likes the feel of a power tool in his hands and who has the imagination to want to do more with it than repairing a closet or a shelf. Wood carving as outlined in the following pages requires no unusual artistic talent, no special skill, no formal training. Even familiarity with power tools isn't important—there is no magic to operating a power tool. What will help you, however, is a willingness to experiment with the wood you are using, for there are no blueprints to follow, very few rules to remember, and no measurements to take. It is entirely freehand, and you are entirely on your own. You don't even have to decide ahead of time what to carve, for the shape of the wood will largely determine this. If you follow the procedure of making a carving as described in this book—a procedure that might be called the natural way, since you will be co-operating with what nature has already put there—it is entirely possible that the *less you know about carving and everything connected with it,* the easier it will be for you to proceed, and the more original and fresh will be your results.

It will be shown in the illustrations that the best and most natural way to make a wood carving is to select carefully a piece of wood that in its natural state so vividly suggests a form—fish, bird, animal, etc.—that only a minimum amount of work will be necessary to realize the finished carving. In the illustrations of carvings that follow, it will be shown that the basic outline or form of the carving was already clearly present in the piece of wood before work was begun. This means that the actual selection of the wood for the carving is about as important as what you do with it. It also means that most of the energy involved in making the carving will be in the illustrations. In most instances you can figure out how to proceed merely by looking at the pictures.

All the carvings and the illustrations of them throughout the book are by the author.

Unless otherwise stated, all carvings were made from cypress wood which was supplied by Cyril Hinds of Lafayette, Louisiana.

Finally, there seems to be some hesitation or even a mild prejudice against using power tools for making a carving, perhaps on the ground that it might give the carving a machine-made look; or, stating it another way, the use of power tools may rob the carving of a personal or individualistic touch. If you were using huge power machines this might be true (a lathe, for example), but this is not the case here. It is still your hand and eye that must guide the grinder or power gun.

A greater reluctance or prejudice may arise in allowing the forms of nature—the shape or outline of the wood—to dominate or to dictate the final form of the carving.

This, of course, is ridiculous; it is the finished carving that counts and not the manner in which it was made. If you make a good carving, that is all that matters. How you made it is not of the slightest importance.

A carving of a toothpick can be made very easily out of an old-fashioned kitchen match. Would it be a better toothpick carving if you had started with or used a fence post instead of a match?

The Illustrations

The photographs obviously were posed. This was done because it was found to be the best way of obtaining a clear picture to illustrate the process of making a carving. The manner in which the photographs were posed is, with one exception, the exact manner in which the carvings were made. This one exception is the occasional awkward way in which the power tools are held in the hand. But this was done in order to get the cutting accessory into the picture. Had the power tool been held in the normal way, it and the hand holding it would have blotted out the cutting accessory.

For the same reason, it was virtually impossible to illustrate the use of the saw and certain positions of the $\frac{1}{4}$-inch drill. The hands before the camera blotted out the carving.

It must also be apparent that the carvings were not made where they were photographed. Instead, they were made on a workbench nearby, and then, along with the tools used, were shifted to where the photographs were taken. Why? Because in spite of the nuisance of dismantling and disconnecting all the power tools each time and shifting them along with the carvings to the camera, it was found that this was still better and easier than trying to adjust the lights and camera to the carvings and tools. In other words, to get a fairly clear picture, the lights and camera were kept stationary, and the carvings and tools were brought to them.

Where both of the author's hands appear in the photographs, the picture was snapped with the foot pressing on a rubber bulb at the end of an extension cable.

Tools, Equipment, and Materials

Even though the tools and equipment in this chapter have been kept to the bare minimum, the reader may well ask after reading it—is it worth it? Are the carvings worth all this outlay in money for tools? The answer definitely is yes, and for two reasons. First, the pleasure derived from making a single good carving is worth the price alone, and yet there is virtually no limit to the number of carvings that you can make with them. Second, the actual outlay in cash isn't nearly as great as you may think. Most homes or workshops already have all the tools in Fig. 1 or reasonable facsimiles. The same applies for the ¼-inch drill in Fig. 20. This tool is standard equipment in any workshop and is a handy tool to have around the house. It has any number of uses besides making a carving, and chances are you already have one. So this leaves only the hand grinder and accessories to buy, which, to begin with, are not too expensive. The hand grinder, too, has many uses in the workshop, besides making wood carvings. So the outlay in cash for tools is really very nominal. Especially is this true when you consider what can be accomplished with them.

As far as the Plastic Wood and lacquer are concerned, it's possible that these materials will not interest you; there are many craftsmen who think it nothing short of a felony to alter the natural surface of the wood with color. If you're one of these, skip those sections. By and large, the author agrees. Keep the carving as simple as possible and let the natural wood speak for itself. However, there will be craftsmen who think otherwise, and who will want to experiment with inlay work, so instructions for the use of these materials have been included.

Roughing-Out Tools

Roughing out a carving means eliminating that part of the wood which you are positive must be removed to free the carving you have in mind. In all the sketches in the chapters that follow, it generally means removing all wood marked X. The four tools pictured in Fig. 1 are all you require to accomplish this. Nor do you necessarily have to use the exact tools shown. For example, any saw you have around will do; and the same applies for the other tools. But these tools do represent maximum efficiency in their respective categories.

The saw shown is about as efficient for removing surplus wood as anything on the market. It cuts with or against the grain with equal ease. In fact, it works so well, that if there is the slightest doubt or hesitation about what you are doing, don't use it. Use the rasp instead. This wood rasp is as coarse as any you can find, and it, too, is very good for removing surplus wood. But, unlike the saw, it still is slow enough to give you a chance to change your mind. The saw does not. The wood gouge is 1 inch and is of imported English steel. It and the hatchet have been tempered and then honed to razor sharpness. Use this wood gouge to remove surplus wood that you cannot get at with the rasp and saw. The use of the hatchet will be discussed later.

Once you gain some experience and self-confidence in clearly visualizing your carving in the piece of wood before you, this roughing-out process will take but a short time. You will have no trouble at all if you follow the suggestions in Chapter 2, and carefully fit or literally squeeze your proposed carving into the shape of the piece of wood before you. Naturally, the more you do this, the less surplus wood there is to remove with the four tools in Fig. 1. You will be using them only in this step. Power tools will be used to finish your carving.

Putting a razor edge on a tool such as a hatchet, chisel, or wood gouge is a craft in itself. This is particularly true of the wood gouge. Since you are going to use these tools only for roughing-out purposes, you will not be using them too often, so perhaps it isn't worth your trying to sharpen them yourself. Every city, town, and even village has a craftsman who specializes in sharpening tools—knives, scissors, axes, and in the winter, ice skates —and who does good work for a comparatively small fee. At the most, these roughing-out tools will have to be sharpened only about once or twice a year, so let one of these craftsmen do it for you.

Of course, if you have a lot of tools around in your workshop, you can use as many as you like in this roughing-out

process. The point is to get rid of the surplus wood in order to realize the carving you have in mind.

With the possible exception of the imported wood gouge, each of these tools can be purchased in any hardware store. If the hardware store near you does not have imported wood gouges, a domestic one, $\frac{3}{4}$ of an inch or 1 inch will do.

$\frac{1}{4}$-inch Drill and Accessories

The tools in Fig. 2 represent the minimum necesary to make all the carvings that follow. The $\frac{1}{4}$-inch drill is a Black and Decker. An important point to keep in mind if you are buying a $\frac{1}{4}$-inch drill is its weight. You will be using this drill a great deal, especially for sanding, so buy the lightest one that you can find. A heavy one will only tire you. Resting on the drill is a 6-inch rubber sponge backing pad manufactured by Carborundum. It is called a Flexbac pad. This backing pad, like the other sanding accessories, is indispensable. You must have these accessories and learn how to use them.

To the right of the drill is a $\frac{3}{8}$-inch wood auger for removing surplus wood by drilling it out. Next to it is a small, coarse sanding drum which has been twisted onto an arbor. The other end of the arbor, of course, is tightened into the $\frac{1}{4}$-inch drill. Next to the sanding drum is a polishing stone or abrasive mounted on a $\frac{1}{4}$-inch shaft which is fitted into the drill. Next to it is a rubber backing pad which has been cut down with a razor from the standard 5-inch size. Why and how this was done is shown in a later illustration. Finally, in the drill itself is a $\frac{1}{4}$-inch bit for drilling holes into your carvings in order to mount them on a base. All these tools will be discussed in detail when they are used to demonstrate a procedure.

Elaborate instructions accompany these tools when you purchase them. Study these instructions and suggestions. If you're still in doubt concerning the proper tool to buy, ask the hardware man who is selling it to you. Don't hesitate to ask questions—they will save you time and money. If you explain exactly what you intend to use a given tool for, your local hardware dealer can supply you with all the information you need. He can also advise you on how much you should spend, and, based on the author's personal experience, the price he suggests rarely will be excessive. Any of these tools, with the possible exception of the small, coarse sanding drums, can be purchased in any hardware store. There isn't too much demand for these small sanding drums, so you may have to write directly to the company manufacturing them or have your local dealer do so. Insist on Black and Decker sanding drums for reasons given in the next chapter. (Black and Decker manufactures an abrasive kit that contains all the sanding accessories that you will require.)

Never buy a power tool on the spur of the moment. Instead, write to companies which manufacture power tools, study their well-illustrated catalogs carefully, and only then decide what to buy and what price to pay.

Additional Accessories

Six-inch sanding discs for the Flexbac sanding pad come in three grades: coarse, medium, and fine. You will seldom have use for the coarse, because the medium is coarse enough for most sanding. But you will want a finer grade than the fine disc. Since the above three grades are the only ones on the market, you will have to make your own.

Take a sheet of very fine garnet paper —7/0 or 8/0 (actually there is very little difference between these two grades, so either will do; but the 8/0 is the finest)— and using a disc that comes with the sanding kit, trace a disc on the garnet paper with a pencil (Fig. 3). Use the thin, plain garnet paper, not the waterproof or any other heavy type; these latter are brittle and will crack.

Now with a razor which has been fastened into a handle, cut the garnet paper along the penciled line as in Fig. 4. The gadget being used is a General. This tool comes in many shapes and is a handy one to have around; instead of bothering to sharpen it, you simply change the blades.

Next press the Flexbac pad down on the garnet paper disc (Fig. 5). This garnet paper will overlap anywhere from 1/8 to 1/4 of an inch. Try to center the Flexbac pad on the garnet disc so that the overlapping is uniform all around.

Press or fold the overlapping edges of the garnet disc back over the edge of the Flexbac pad (Fig. 6).

This enables you to sand uphill as shown in Fig. 7, or in corners. If you were using a regular stiff sanding disc it would cut into the wood. The soft garnet paper with the slightly folded edge does not.

Remember in sanding that it is the action of the disc that does the work and not the pressure. Therefore, don't put too much pressure on the tool or you will tear the garnet paper. In sanding—especially in finishing the carving—the lighter the touch the better.

There will often be occasions—when there is only a little work to be done—when you will not bother to fasten your carving in the vise but will rasp, sand, or carve with the power tools while holding the carving on the workbench or on your knees. Always take the precaution of protecting yourself by wearing a heavy canvas apron folded in half (Fig. 8). It is excellent protection against a possible accident and should be worn at all times. If you cannot find such an apron, take two strips of heavy canvas and have a shoemaker or a tailor stitch them on a pair of work pants as in Fig. 9. Power tools and tools in general are not dangerous if common sense is used and this means taking your time. Do not try to hurry a carving along either with hand tools or with power tools. The author over the past few years has made hundreds of carvings, and, except for an occasional scratch, usually in using the wood rasp, has never injured himself.

Following are a few suggestions concerning hand tools: watch your free hand in using the saw, especially the coarse-toothed saw depicted in Fig. 1, in guiding the blade at the start. When using the hatchet, keep your body well away in case the hatchet blade should glance. Never, but never, under any circumstances should you hold your wood carving in one hand and attempt to carve it by holding the chisel or wood gouge in the other. This is an almost certain way to invite trouble. Never use the wood gouge unless your carving is firmly fastened in the vise.

When using power tools, avoid loose clothing which might get caught in the cutting accessory. Should anything go wrong, learn where the switch is in order to cut off the power tool or better still drop it. You may injure it and the accessory slightly, but that is better than injuring yourself.

Hand Grinder and Accessories

If you are planning on buying a hand grinder, first write to the companies manufacturing them and study their catalogs carefully. They are very well illustrated and you can take your time about making up your mind both as to the type of grinder you require and the price you wish to pay.

The hand grinder in Fig. 10 and six accessories are entirely adequate to make all but the largest carvings that follow. This hand grinder—a popular model—is manufactured by Chicago Wheel and Manufacturing Co. There is at least one other make (Dremel) on the market, that is undoubtedly just as good.

The five accessories above the hand grinder from left to right are: a small polishing stone; a large high-speed rotary file or cutter; a large burr; a medium burr; and a small burr. In the hand grinder is a smaller version of the high-speed rotary file or cutter. All these and countless other accessories are in the manufacturer's catalogs, with suggestions for using them. Not every hardware store stocks these accessories. Or it is possible that the particular one you want will not be in stock. Rather than accept a substitute, order directly from the company. These accessories are numbered and easy to order. Always insist on the high-speed variety. They cost more, but they are well worth it because they do not dull nearly as quickly as the regular.

You will notice that other hand grinders —a Dumore hand grinder and a Foredom flexible-shaft hand grinder—are used in making the carvings besides the Handee grinder.

This in no way alters what has been said about the Handee being entirely adequate to make the smaller carvings. These other grinders were used both to illustrate that there are other grinders on the market and also to point out that some hand grinders have certain advantages over others (also disadvantages).

The Dumore hand grinder is, of course, much heavier than the Handee and more difficult to guide or control, especially with one hand. As a matter of fact, this tool was not designed to be used with one hand. Yet, there will be many occasions when you will do so. For heavy work, such as grooving large carvings, it has few if any equals on the market. But for detail work such as carving in the eye of an animal or bird, it is almost too powerful and too difficult to guide. One false move with this powerhouse and you might

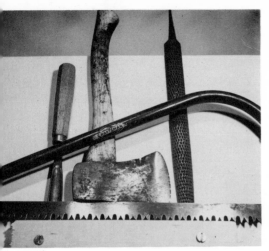

FIG. 1

FIG. 2

FIG. 3

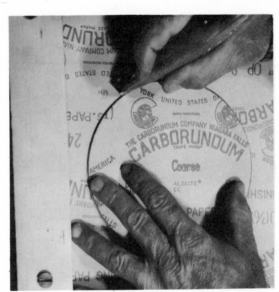

FIG. 4

FIG. 5

FIG. 6

Fig. 7

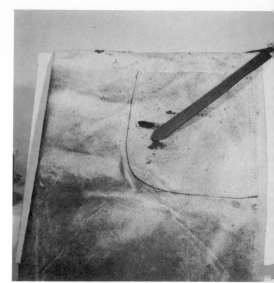

Fig. 8

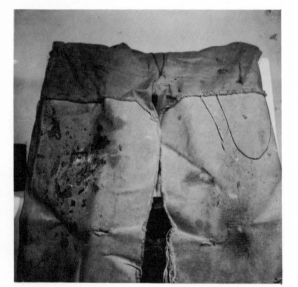

Fig. 9

Fig. 10

Fig. 11

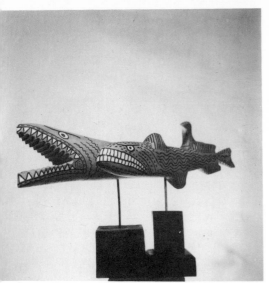

FIG. 12

FIG. 13

FIG. 14

FIG. 15

have to begin work all over again on a new carving.

The Foredom flexible-shaft grinder like the Handee is entirely adequate for small carvings and detail work. Being a flexible-shaft grinder, it is even easier to handle; carving with it is almost exactly like holding a pen or pencil in your hand. Yet, when it comes to heavy work, it is no match for the Dumore hand grinder.

The ideal grinder is one that has all the power that you are ever likely to need, one that is easy to handle so as not to tire you, and one that is easy to guide for fine detail work. Undoubtedly, this is the Power Flex or the Super Flex manufactured by Dumore Precision Tools. With either one of these models, you can do anything that the three grinders do which are used throughout the book—heavy work or fine detail. Since this a flexible-shaft grinder, you can operate it without tiring. With a foot rheostat to control the power, this is the one perfect grinder for power-tool carving. A glance through any of the mechanical magazines will give you the addresses of these power-tool companies. Write for their catalogs.

All companies manufacturing power tools—hand grinders, flexible-shaft tools, ¼-inch drills—make these tools in different sizes, shapes, models, power, etc. Determine what model best suits the type of carving you intend to make. This refers mostly to the size of your carving, and how involved the work will be. Don't look for bargains in hand grinders, or any other power tool for that matter. Stick to recognized and established name brands. If you don't, you are almost certain to be disappointed. Don't handicap yourself with inferior tools. Buying name brands means that you're usually on the safe side. But there are exceptions. Tools like a screw driver, a hammer, a paintbrush, etc., or any other tool that you will use only infrequently, can be of a cheaper variety,

and they are as effective as more expensive models.

Materials Needed to Inlay a Carving with Plastic Wood and Liquid Metals

Pictured in Fig. 11 are about as many different colors of Plastic Wood as are available. The can behind the pallet knife is gumwood. Few hardware stores stock all these colors, but they should have light and dark mahogany and walnut. These colors are sufficient to make a start. In Chapter 11, "Inlaying with Plastic Wood," suggestions will be made on how to color your own inlay material, using the natural Plastic Wood as a base. Also shown in Fig. 11 are a pallet knife, wax, and Plastic Wood Solvent.

Liquid metals can also be used for inlay work. There are many on the market, including liquid iron. Pictured are a tube of liquid solder and a tube of aluminum. You can ignore the solder because it is unsatisfactory, but the aluminum is excellent.

In Fig. 12, you see two angry fish which have been inlaid. Chapter 11 demonstrates exactly how these results were achieved.

Materials Needed to Inlay a Carving with Melted Lacquer

The color of the six lacquer sticks between the small torch—used to melt the colors—and the pair of pliers are green, red, blue, white, black, and yellow (Fig. 13). These sticks come in many shades of each color. Yet, for a beginning, the brightest color of each will do. These sticks are brittle and break up easily. Therefore, you will need a pair of pliers to hold the small pieces to the torch. How to apply the color is shown in the illustrations in Chapter 10, "Lacquering." Once applied, these colors resemble glass or ceramic. The lacquer dries and hardens almost instantly, and the colors are very brilliant. Inlaying with this material—lacquer in sticks—and with this method—using wood as an armature—produces some very startling results.

The color is easy to apply, although difficult to control. It is also reasonably permanent, because some carvings done by the author which were inlaid several years ago are the same today. An illustration of such a piece is in Chapter 7, in the section entitled, "A Bird Form in the Round."

Sticks of hard color that must be melted with a torch are also available in porcelain, marble, and, of course, shellac. However, in these other products, the choice of color is more limited and, since they are very similar in application, only lacquer will be discussed. Also, once applied, it is very difficult to tell which is which. There are no green, yellow, red, or blue shellac sticks. These latter come only in white and black, and the various colors of wood such as oak, mahogany, walnut, etc. With the exception of the shellac sticks, few, if any, hardware stores carry these items. A large paint store might carry a few colors of lacquer, but more than likely if you wish to experiment with this method, you will have to order the material through the mail. The lacquer sticks in the illustration came from H. Behlen and Bro., Inc., 10 Christopher Street, New York, New York. They have a small folder listing by number the various colors of lacquer available and will gladly send you one. The small torch and refills for the torch can be purchased in any hardware store. Any pair of pliers will do.

Figure 14 shows a carving of a young girl being inlaid with black and white lacquer. Step-by-step illustrations of how this was done are shown in Chapter 10, "Lacquering."

Materials Needed to Finish a Carving

Before waxing your carving, give it a coat or two of Firzite cut 50-50 with benzine. This mixture tends to seal the pores of the wood without giving it a cheap gloss, and it dries quickly. After it is thoroughly dry, sand lightly by hand with a 7/0 or an 8/0 garnet paper and then wax. This procedure cuts the amount of wax you would have to use to get a high polish about in half, because naturally any soft wood and especially cross sections of soft wood soak up the wax like a sponge. You don't have to use Firzite. A clear shellac cut with alcohol will do the same thing. So will lacquer cut with lacquer thinner. The important thing is to avoid the cheap gloss that any of these products (see Fig. 15) might give your carving if they are not cut.

However, should this gloss appear in spite of your efforts to avoid it (applying too much will do it), it is easier to remove by rubbing the carving with the pure cutting agent than by trying to sand it off. You might well wonder just what is the difference between a high polish achieved with wax and the gloss achieved with the above products. There is a very big difference. The gloss makes the carving look amateurish and reduces the carving to the level of a toy.

If your carving is in a hardwood and if the over-all design is very simple, you might give it what can be called a simulated French finish. Give it a light coat of any of the above mixtures, either with a paintbrush (the inexpensive variety will do), or you can use a piece of cloth. Allow the coating to dry thoroughly, and then sand either with a 8/0 garnet paper or very fine steel wool. Do this by hand. Remember that what gives a carving a French-finish look is work—plenty of rubbing, nothing else. And there is no short cut. Now, perform this operation at least six or eight times. Toward the end, you might even try rubbing the carving with a very fine powder. If nothing else is available, a woman's face powder will do.

If you rub hard and long enough, your carving will gradually take on the appearance of a fence post or the corner of a barn where livestock over the years have been rubbing or scratching themselves. This involves a lot of work, but if you have a carving you value highly, it is well worth it. Naturally, you don't have to wax or do anything else to such a carving. However, if this process seems like too much work, or if you decide your carving does not warrant it, you can cut the work about in half by applying several coats of wax after three or four applications of the above mixtures. You will still have to rub the carving between each application.

Perhaps you don't want your carving to have a high polish. Then, after a thorough sanding, give it a coat or two of linseed oil. Be sure to rub the surplus off well or it will collect dust.

If your carving looks good as is—that is, in the natural wood—don't bother to use stain. Anyway, it is unlikely that you will ever have occasion to use as much stain as is in the containers in Fig. 15. If you wish to experiment, a very small can will do. The two cans pictured are walnut and red mahogany. Explain to the paint dealer what you intend to use the stain for and, of course, what kind of wood you intend to stain. He will offer you some suggestions.

Perhaps your carving doesn't require a finish at all. If so, leave it in the rough. This rule applies particularly if the tool marks are left on the carving. In this connection, where your carving has not been waxed or treated with any other mixture, it would be interesting to see what the weather would do to it. You might try leaving such a carving—if it is in very soft wood—out in the sun and rain for some months, or perhaps a year, and see what happens.

A carving, well burnished, needs no other finish. Also, perhaps your carving will look best if just given a very light coat of wax without any rubbing or polishing. The best way to find out is to experiment.

Wood

What Wood to Use and Where to Get It

One of the best woods for power-tool carving is the root of the cypress tree, more commonly known as the cypress knee. Its color ranges from ivory to a reddish brown. It is very easy to carve, light to handle, and takes a high polish. It is so fibrous that it will take any amount of detail; and, by working with the grain, it can be carved to razor thinness. Pictured in Fig. 16 are cypress knees as they are sawed in the swamp. At this stage, they are water soaked and heavy. These knees average about 2 feet in height, and the largest is about 8 to 10 inches across the bottom. Each of these will weigh about 25 pounds when cut.

The knees can be dried out merely by placing them in the sun in the position shown, except that they should be raised off the ground in order to allow the air to circulate and also to allow the moisture to drain out. Be careful, though, not to expose them to too much sun or to too hot a sun immediately after they are cut because they may crack. However, once properly dried out, a cypress knee will rarely, if ever, check. Temperature changes appear to have little or no effect on cypress. To get an idea how permanent cypress wood is and how much abuse it can take from the weather, one has only to recall that there are still numerous buildings around whose roofs were shingled with cypress 50 or even 100 years ago. Few if any other woods can equal this. In other words, once you've made a carving out of a properly dried-out piece of cypress, you have little cause to worry about it ever checking no matter what temperature changes or conditions it is subjected to.

If it does not affect the carving the knee is intended for, the drying-up process can be speeded up by drilling a hole up into the knee from the bottom about 8 or 10 inches. If this is done shortly after the knee is cut, the water actually will run out. Once they are dried out properly, these roots weigh but a few pounds. Some cypress knees are almost as light as balsa wood.

Figure 17 shows cypress knees after the bark has been removed by steaming. This should be done as soon after the knee is cut as possible. After steaming for 30 minutes or an hour, the bark strips off easily. The knees in the illustration are thoroughly dry and ready for carving.

Cypress wood is amazing in that you virtually can do anything with it with power tools. Since the bark is already removed, it is easy to sketch on with chalk or charcoal. No two of these cypress knees are alike, and some of them, as you will see from the illustrations, are truly weird. Don't forget to allow the particular shape of the knee to determine the carving.

There are men in the Gulf States who

cut, remove the bark, season these knees and then sell them for souvenirs or for decorations or to people who wish to make lamps out of them. Many sell them along the highways to tourists, as anyone who has traveled through the Gulf States knows. Most of these roadside stands are in the State of Florida. Some of them, on occasion, advertise in the classified advertisement sections of the mechanical, and hobby or craftsmen magazines. As a rule, their ads appear under the home craftsman or hobby classifications. One man in Florida, Thomas Gaskins, has built a museum near Palmdale, where only cypress knees are exhibited.

If you think you might be interested in carving cypress knees, perhaps the Florida Chamber of Commerce can supply you with the addresses of some places that sell them. These cypress knees damage and bruise very easily when first cut. This lessens their value as a souvenir or a decoration, yet does not make the slightest difference if you are going to carve them. In writing, be sure to mention that you intend to use the knee for carving purposes; you then may be able to purchase it at a cheaper price than if it were not bruised or damaged. The price depends entirely on the size and on how fantastic the shape is. Of course, anyone living in the South can go out and select and cut his own cypress knees. In a city like New Orleans, Louisiana (and there must be many others), you scarcely have to leave the city limits.

Logs or any odd-shaped piece of wood found in a lumberyard or forest also can be used. Power tools are used to do the actual carving, so it doesn't matter how hard the wood is. Remember, the odder or weirder the shape of the piece of wood, the better. If it is solid, dry, and free from large cracks, you can always figure out some carving to fit into it. Often on a hike through the forest, or along a lake or river, or the sea coast, a piece of drift-wood, a large branch, or the small trunk of a tree with an interesting curve or twist or odd shape can be found that will immediately suggest some carving to you. It is entirely possible that only a minimum amount of work on your part will be necessary to bring out the carving. The basic form is already there. All you do is to free it. Surely this is the best way to make a start at wood carving. All it takes is a little intelligent collaboration with what nature has already put there. By all odds, this is easier and more interesting than trying to make a carving out of a square block of wood. In fact, the search for the wood can be as interesting as the carving.

Additional comments concerning wood will be made as the different woods are carved, and also suggestions as to where to get the wood.

Where to Get Ideas

The best source for ideas is the shape of the wood itself. Study carefully the piece you intend to carve, arranging it in different positions until it suggests something to you. Then take advantage of the shape of the wood and literally squeeze into it the form it suggests. The more you do this, the less wood you will have to remove to realize the form. This letting the shape of the wood suggest the carving is very important, for it means working with the wood and not fighting it. It also means that usually you will be working with the grain of the wood. This is not really difficult if you approach the piece of wood without any preconceived ideas, and you are willing to go along with the shape before you.

Co-operating with the wood is the best way to proceed. The style you use to free the form is entirely up to you. The best way is to go about it in your own way (trial and error), instead of looking for advice from books or persons. Alone you might develop a new and original style. At least you will have the satisfaction of knowing the finished carving is entirely your own. Certainly there is then every possibility that your carving will be different from others. If you use the trial-and-error method, it is wise to have plenty of wood around so that spoiling a piece while experimenting will not become an issue. If you only have one or two pieces of costly wood, you are going to be cautious or conservative, and that is no way to experiment. In the beginning, keep your carvings small, because small pieces are easier to control, and they require less time and effort to finish.

If you find this freehand method difficult and if you are interested in nature, there are inexpensive pocket editions of books on birds, animals, fishes, and plants that will serve as a guide, since all you're interested in is a vague impression anyway. In making a carving of a bird or fish, do not try to compete with the taxidermist. It will help if you regard your carvings as bird or fish forms and not try to duplicate any particular bird or fish. Familiarize yourself with the pictures in these books, and you'll have no trouble deciding what form to fit into the wood you intend to carve.

Any book dealing with primitive art, with emphasis on the African, South Seas (Maori), American Indian (Pacific Northwest), Mexican, or Central American, is a rich source for ideas for wood carvings. Where these primitive carvings, both wood and stone, can help you is not so much in their subject matter, as in the manner of carving (style, surface treatment, decorations). For example, an African Negro carving or a Maori carving may not interest you, but a careful study of the manner in which it was made can teach you a great deal. This is especially true of the fantastic designs and details a Maori achieves. While his detail would be extraordinarily difficult to adopt by hand, it is relatively simple with power tools.

Books on the ancient art of the Far East and the Middle East are other good sources of ideas. Don't hesitate to let yourself be influenced by primitive or ancient art. Almost every important modern sculptor and many modern painters owe much to ancient or primitive art. Finally, don't overlook early American wood carving.

Seeing the Carving in the Wood

Seeing the carving in the wood is largely a matter of practice, a little imagination, and common sense—mainly common sense. You allow yourself to be guided by the shape of wood you are using and not by any preconceived ideas you might have. If the wood you are using suggests a fish, then carve a fish. Do not try to carve a bird or animal out of it. If you wish to carve a bird or animal, then look for another piece of wood that suggests a bird or animal.

The grain of the wood in a carving, especially a fish carving, can be equally as important as the shape of the wood; but rather than complicate matters now, this will be taken up in Chapter 4. For the present, concentrate only on the shape of the wood.

The main thing to remember here is to have an open mind. Forget everything else and concentrate on the wood. Shift it around in different positions until it suggests some form to you, always keeping in mind that you are going to try to utilize as much of the shape of the wood as possible. The more you do this, the less wood you will have to remove to realize the form and, of course, this means less work. This point will be illustrated clearly in the illustrations that follow.

Begin your sketching with a sharpened piece of white chalk, or a charcoal pencil or stick. The marks can be wiped off with a damp cloth should you decide to alter

Fig. 16

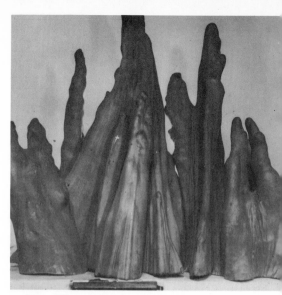

Fig. 17

Fig. 18

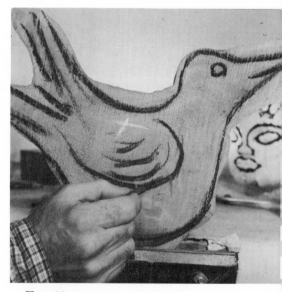

Fig. 19

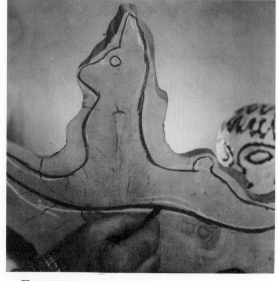

Fig. 20

Fig. 21

the sketch. Charcoal sticks are very inexpensive, and they are as good as anything. Once you are fairly certain of what you intend to carve, go over the sketch with a black crayon, a soft lead carpenter's pencil, or an ink marker to make your sketch more permanent. Do not use an ink marker when the carving is nearing completion, because the ink penetrates the wood. Use a soft lead pencil instead.

Unless otherwise stated, all discs of wood are about an inch or less thick, and the width and height can be gauged by the size of the hand in the illustrations, so no measurements will be given unless they seem necessary. These discs or cross sections were sawed off the end of various-shaped cypress knees or roots.

The Cross Sections

Regardless of the shape of the piece of wood before you, always remember that there are any number of other carvings that can be fitted into it besides the first or more obvious one that comes to your mind. For example, the fish sketch in Fig. 18 is not interesting, but, if you turn this disc of wood around—Fig. 19—a bird form can be fitted into it. This bird form is not only more interesting, but it fits into the shape of the wood better. Except for the wood around the bill of the bird, there is very little to remove. What there is can be rasped off. To complete this carving, all you have to do is gradually round the sharp edges with the wood rasp and then sand thoroughly. These discs are no heavier than a picture frame of the same size, so they can be hung on a wall.

The cross section in Fig. 20 is about 2 inches thick, and, although the sketch would make a fair carving, it will not be made because too much wood would be wasted. Instead some other carving will be fitted into the wood.

Again, Figure 21 is not an interesting fish form, but turn it around so the fish

sketch is sitting on its tail, and you can sketch in a baby penguin—Fig. 22—which is more exciting.

Notice in contrast to the sketch in Fig. 20 how the two sketches in Figs. 23 and 24 fill the outline of the disc, and how little wood would have to be removed to realize the carving.

The disc in Fig. 25 is at least 2 inches thick, which means that the fish form sketched on it could be carved "in the round." A carving in the round means, of course, that the entire fish could be carved and not just a silhouette. Unlike the other two fish sketches, this one is fairly interesting; it conveys the impression of motion.

Now turn this disc around and set it on the fish's head, and you have a squirrel form (Fig. 26). A carving of a squirrel in the round could also be squeezed into this disc, and either sketch would result in an intriguing carving, making it difficult to decide which to carve. That the fish sketch in Fig. 25 is not true to nature is not important. It is the suggestion of motion that gives the sketch merit.

Notice how the two roots in Figs. 27 and 28 come to a gradual point. Yet, the basic or general outline of the wood remains the same. This means that if you cut ten 1-inch discs off these roots, the tenth one would naturally be much smaller than the first one, but, and this is the point, *in all other respects they would be more or less the same.* Now you have ten discs, each one a bit smaller than the other, although in all other respects almost identical. You don't need too much imagination to realize what an unusual wood mural you could make out of these ten discs. Properly spaced, these tropical fish forms would stretch across a 20-foot wall space. As each one is slightly smaller than the previous one, perspective could be introduced into the design—arrange the mural on the wall at an angle so that the smaller fish forms gradually would

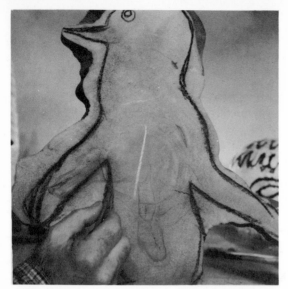

FIG. 22

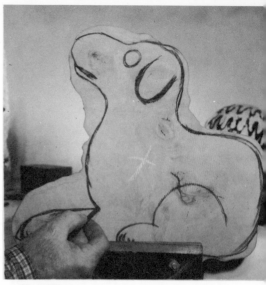

FIG. 23

FIG. 24

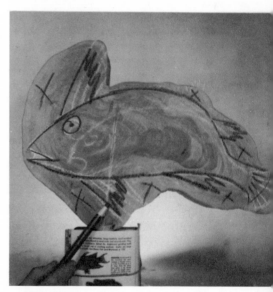

FIG. 25

FIG. 26

FIG. 27

Fig. 28

Fig. 29

Fig. 30

Fig. 31

Fig. 32

Fig. 33

21

FIG. 34

FIG. 35

FIG. 36

FIG. 37

FIG. 38

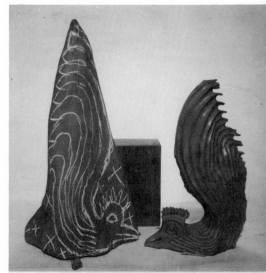

FIG. 39

22

FIG. 40

FIG. 41

FIG. 42

FIG. 43

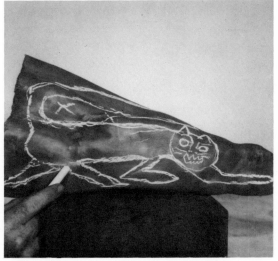

FIG. 44

disappear into a corner of the ceiling. At any rate, to make a wall mural like this, using regular lumber, would not only involve a great deal of work, but it would also be costly because of the enormous amount of wood which would be wasted. Yet here there is no more work involved than sawing off the discs—the fish form is there already. In a project like this, at least 50 per cent or more of the work has already been done by nature. Both these roots are more than 40 inches tall and measure about 25 inches across the base at their widest part.

Figure 29 shows the sketched fish of Fig. 28 being burnished with a stone abrasive in the power drill. Once the carving is burnished, it will be waxed thoroughly.

Figure 30 proves that there is scarcely a cross section of a tree or branch or root, no matter how weird, that you cannot, with a little imagination, fit a fish form into.

In the Round

The same piece of wood was used to make the sketches in Figs. 31 through 42. Notice how many different forms literally can be squeezed into this one piece of wood. Looked at from the bottom, the wood resembles a triangle or a pyramid.

In the three duck carvings (Figs. 31–33), the head and neck of the duck fills the top part of this triangle or pyramid; the body of the duck fills the base. In all the carvings of animals, the tail fills this top part and the body of the animal fills the base of the wood.

In almost all these sketches, the wood marked X can be removed with a saw. You have then only to round the sharp edges with a rasp and your form is roughed out and ready for carving.

In the animals, the wood marked X between the tail and the body of the animal can be drilled out with a $\frac{1}{2}$-inch wood auger in the $\frac{1}{4}$-inch drill and then rasped. In any one of these sketches, notice how very little wood has to be removed to realize the form. These sketches show how about 14 different forms can be carved from a single piece of wood. The rabbit in Fig. 43, although sketched on a different piece of wood, could also have been fitted into this same piece, in which case the head and ears of the rabbit would fill the top part of the pyramid and the body, the base. The angry cat in Fig. 44 is also sketched on a different piece of wood, but this, too, could have been fitted into the above.

Making Your First Carving

The carvings in this chapter are meant as an exercise and not as finished work. Regard them in the same way that you would if you were sketching on a pad, except that here, instead of charcoal or a pencil, you are using power tools, and instead of a scratch pad you are using wood. If the carving does not turn out as you had hoped, set it to one side or discard it, the same as you would discard the scratch paper, and start over again on a brand-new piece.

It is not merely a matter of learning how to use power tools—this is easy, as the instructions that accompany the power tools can tell you—it is rather a matter of becoming so familiar with power tools that they become a natural extension of your hand in exactly the same way that a pencil does when you write a letter. Whatever mental effort goes into writing a letter goes into the contents of the letter and not into the manual manipulation of the pencil. If you can write at all, this comes naturally. It is the same with learning how to use power tools. When you reach a point where all your efforts are directed mainly at what you are carving and not to the power tools in your hand, then, like the pencil or a typewriter, the power tool has become an extension of your hand. This can only come about through actual work and a lot of practice. This accounts for the almost endless repetition that follows, for, surely, repeating

the same thing over and over is one of the best ways to learn.

Anyone who knows how to use power tools, or learns how, can make the carvings in the book. Without exception, they are very simple to make. It does not matter if you have never made a carving before or even thought about it. If you have the power tools and, just as important, *if you start with the right piece of wood*, you can make these carvings. There must be many of you craftsmen who have the power tools and the workshop but who are weary of making bookcases, birdhouses, etc. It is hoped that this book might get you started in a new direction, one you probably just never thought of before.

Most people like gadgets, especially laborsaving gadgets. There is a fascination in just the feel of the hand grinder while it is operating. Some of this fascination is undoubtedly due to the fact that it is electricity which is furnishing the energy and not yourself. This should appeal to teen-agers, not because they don't like work, but because most of them are fascinated by mechanical gadgets. Perhaps some of the suggestions and illustrations here will help them get started in an interesting hobby. Most of the carvings are small. A small workshop with a small workbench will do.

Don't take yourself or your carving too seriously, because this will have a tendency to make you hesitant and conservative; and this is no mood to be in when you are learning. Worrying or fondling the carving along might be the correct approach if you were trying to produce a masterpiece of wood sculpture, but it is assumed in this chapter that you are just getting started.

Before making a carving, examine all the illustrations in this book, for there may be a suggestion with the accompanying text that will be of help in making your first carving. Furthermore, by just looking at the illustrations carefully, you can get a good idea of how to proceed. What may puzzle you in one section may be cleared up in the next. Whatever you carve, the method is the same.

First, take full advantage of the shape of the wood you are using. Do not have any preconceived ideas about what you want to carve, but rather let the shape of the wood determine this. Don't hesitate to change your mind or to experiment if your first sketch doesn't utilize all the wood. With practice, you can learn to do this so well that very little roughing out will be necessary. Most of the carvings illustrated were so carefully fitted into the original shape of the wood that the roughing-out process took but a few minutes.

Second, once you've made up your mind what to carve, use the most efficient tools, the saw and rasp, and do the roughing out quickly.

Third, clean up the carving with the sanding drums and discs in the ¼-inch drill, sketch in your design, and begin carving. For heavy carving, use the large hand grinder with the high-speed rotary files; for fine detail, use the small grinder with small cutters. Keep in mind that it is just as important to learn what a power tool can't do as it is to learn what it can do. No hand grinder on the market can compete with the saw, rasp, chisel, and hatchet when it comes to removing surplus wood.

Finally, remember that the following carvings are sketches to illustrate both the method of carving and the method of utilizing the full shape of the wood you intend to carve.

One of the main problems confronting the carver, especially if he lives in a large city, is where to get wood for carving. Although this matter was discussed in Chapter 2, here are a few more suggestions. If you live in a city, perhaps the man who supplies wood for fireplaces can deliver you one or maybe several unsplit sections of logs. Specify that you want soft woods: white pine, birch, poplar, etc. Also request differently shaped logs so you will have a variety of forms to experiment with. A log, oblong in shape at the butt end, is best—a disc sawed off the end already suggests a fish form. For a beginning, keep your carvings small. All the carvings in this section are about 6 to 8 inches in length, and all are carved from cypress discs.

Most soft woods are common and inexpensive. The problem is to locate them and to transport them to your studio or workshop. Most of the carvings in this section are made from discs which are no more than 1 or 1½ inches in width; thus the cost of each disc should not be very much. You should be able to saw at least 15 discs off a 2-foot section of a log.

Any forest will have dried-out logs or uprooted trees in it. If you live near one, explain to the owner what you intend to use the wood for, and generally he will give you permission to cut what you need. If you are alert and on the lookout, wood can be found in the most unexpected places. Wherever there is highway construction, there is bound to be plenty of wood around. The same applies for any large construction project or where old buildings are being torn down. You know in advance that any wood from these old buildings will be well seasoned.

Collect interesting pieces of wood at every opportunity, even if you have no immediate use for it. The older the wood gets, the easier it is to carve. Remember that any wood that has a pronounced grain is more interesting to carve and will make a more appealing carving. Well-defined age circles on the butt end of the log will indicate if the discs you saw off will have a pronounced grain or not. (Chapter 5 will show you how to stretch out this grain.)

All wood used in this chapter and the next are cross sections or discs sawed off the butt end of cypress knees or roots. Thus you will be carving directly into the grain of the wood, which means that you will be working against the grain and not with it. For this reason, you must have power tools. Certainly it wouldn't be worth the effort to try to make this type of carving with hand tools. It would be enormously difficult, if not actually impossible. With power tools, however, as you will see presently, there is nothing to it. If you are using only hand tools, turn to Chapter 4 where the illustrations demonstrate how to make a fish carving by working *with* the grain of the wood.

Project #1

The sketched fish on the bottom left of Fig. 45 is the fish being carved in this project. The book will give you an idea of the size of these carvings. The two fish carvings directly above the one being carved were sawed off the same cypress root. A close look at the grain of the wood will show this even though the carvings do not look too much alike. These small carvings are not much bigger than your hand and are very easy to make. One or even two can be made in a single evening. You can mount them on a small base or hang them in groups on a wall. All wood marked X in these sketches will be removed, either with a saw or, if that is not

practical, it will be drilled out with a wood auger in the power drill.

In Fig. 46, a 1-inch disc is being sawed off the end of a cypress knee. You don't have to use cypress wood. Any dried-out cross section of a log will do. Since this is only an exercise for you to become acquainted with procedure and how to handle the power tools, use soft wood. In sketching in your fish, use as much of the wood as possible. Study the sketches in these illustrations for ideas. An almost round disc is being used deliberately for the fish carving because this is the commonest shape and the one with which you're most likely to begin.

Balance the carving on your hand or finger and, wherever it balances, drill a hole there (Fig. 47)—¼ inch in width and about 1 inch deep—in order to mount the carving later. Be sure the hole is drilled into the disc at the correct angle. You can determine this by holding the carving on a base in its proper position, and then indicate with a chalk line the direction you are to drill. You will notice this chalk line in most every carving. It is a dependable guide to follow. The wood between the tail and the fins in the carving has been drilled out. The same is true of the mouth of the fish. This carving is now ready for rasping.

Draw a line around the disc in the center. This is to serve as a guide as the carving is gradually rounded or shaped like a fish. An ink marker is being used in Fig. 48, but a crayon or soft pencil will do. An ink marker has been used almost exclusively in the book because it shows up better. Notice how vague the sketching of the fish is. This is deliberate—there is nothing final about it and the shape may be changed as the carving progresses. Never hesitate to change your mind, even after the carving has begun. Remember these carvings are entirely freehand. You are not following any blueprints.

FIG. 45

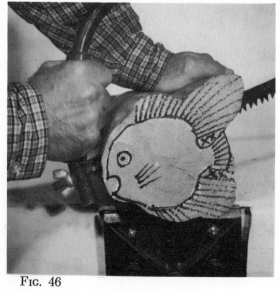

FIG. 46

FIG. 47

As you can tell from the carving in Fig. 49, the wood marked *X* in the previous sketch was removed with a saw.

Naturally a fish, any fish, comes to a gradual point at the head and tail and at the top and bottom. Using a coarse wood rasp, as shown in Fig. 50, shape your carving exactly like the oval used in track meets.

After rasping, go over the carving with a medium sanding disc (Fig. 51). At this stage, sand it smooth enough only to the extent that it is easy to sketch on. The sanding gadget is the Flexbac pad. Complete instructions come with the sanding kit. The wood in this illustration, although it doesn't look like one, is also a disc or cross section. But it is from the cypress tree itself and not the knee or root. How this disc was sawed is shown in Chapter 5, "The Importance of Grain." Of course, any other electric sanding machine you may have can be used to sand the carving. But you must use a sanding gadget powered by electricity, because what you actually are sanding here is the butt end of a log. Surely you're not going to try to do this by hand! After sanding, sketch in the design—eyes, gills, fins, etc.—you intend to carve.

Note: You do not have to buy the Flexbac pad. A rubber backing pad will do for a start. Some sanding kits, besides the rubber backing pad, also include various grades of sanding discs and a polishing bonnet. These sanding kits are slightly more expensive but are well worth the price. However, the Flexbac pad has definite advantages which will be taken up later.

To carve in the eyes (Fig. 52), use a small cutting burr in the hand grinder and lightly trace over the sketched eye. Do not try to make the groove deep, because this will make the grinder harder to control, but rather just scratch the surface of the wood. Also use your free thumb to help guide the grinder exactly as you see it being done in Fig. 53. Now put a medium-sized burr into the grinder and again trace over the eye, making the grooves both wider and deeper—$\frac{1}{16}$ of an inch is deep enough. Remember, the smaller the cutting burr you are using, the easier it is to guide or control.

A Foredom flexible-shaft grinder is being used in Fig. 54. It was also used at some time or other in all the carvings. The reason it does not appear in many of the illustrations is because of the trouble of dismantling it—the motor is suspended from the ceiling—and also because a rheostat or foot control is connected to the grinder. This tool is very similar to what a dentist uses. The rheostat enables you to control the speed of the grinder. The fins or grooves on the carving, bottom right, in Fig. 52 were carved in with the large high-speed rotary file you see in Fig. 54. Although you are cutting directly into the grain of the wood, this rotary file does the job as though the wood were soft butter. Make these grooves the same as you see them made in Fig. 54. The small *xxxx*'s on the carving in Fig. 52 are there only as a guide in taking the picture.

The grooves or fins of the bottom carving in Fig. 55 were sanded with the small sanding drum you see in Fig. 56, and in the same manner as demonstrated.

This little sanding drum can do an amazing amount of work and take an incredible amount of abuse. There is almost no sanding operation that you cannot do with it. As you use it, the end wears down to a point, which means that you can reach even into the smallest corners. These small sanding drums are so tough and so well constructed that just one or two such drums are enough to make a dozen of the carvings, except the very largest. Even after the drum has been worn down to only $\frac{1}{3}$ or $\frac{1}{4}$ its regular size, it still retains its abrasive qualities. There are

Fig. 48

Fig. 49

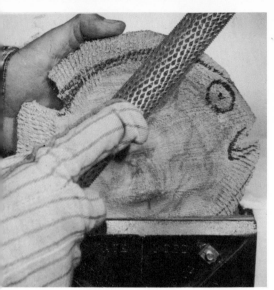

Fig. 50

Fig. 51

Fig. 52

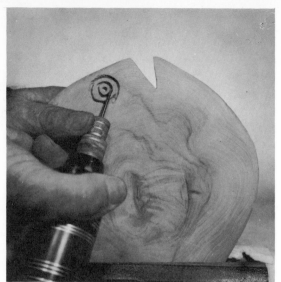

Fig. 53

Fig. 54

Fig. 55

many such drums of various sizes and shapes and qualities on the market. Some are still being sold as war surplus material. Some have the arbor already glued or soldered in the drum. Do not buy any of these latter; they are no bargain. They are apparently made of the very cheapest materials and very poorly put together at that. They are not worth even half the price they sell for. Those with the arbor already soldered into the sanding drum come apart almost immediately, and those which twist or screw onto the arbor tear loose almost as quickly. But what is worse, these sanding drums have no abrasive qualities to start with. So there is no point in buying them.

Note: the arbor is the piece of metal that is tightened into the 1/4-inch drill. The end of this iron bar is shaped like a corkscrew. You fasten the sanding drum to this end. This sanding drum is sandpaper glued together. Make certain that you fasten the drum on the arbor so that it spins in the opposite direction from which it is wrapped. One end of the sanding drum is covered with glue. This is the end to tighten on the arbor.

The sanding drum in these illustrations is manufactured by Black and Decker. It comes in two grades—coarse and fine. In all the illustrations, it is the coarse one that is being used. This seems to do the work satisfactorily, so you will have few occasions to use the fine one. You will use these small sanding drums a great deal, even though they are not pictured too often. In fact, many of these carvings cannot be made without them.

Note: Behr-Manning are manufacturers of abrasives and their abrasive drums probably are as good as the one illustrated here. But the author has never been able to locate one even in a city the size of New York. On the other hand, he has been using the sanding drums made by Black and Decker for years.

If the wood you are using is fairly soft, the abrasive qualities of the coarse drum are such that you can model or shape the wood with it the same as if you were carving with the rotary file. Learn to maneuver the spinning abrasive in various ways over the wood, and you will be amazed at what you can accomplish with it. You don't have to bear down hard on the drum; it is the spinning action that makes it a good abrasive and not the pressure.

Use a small stone abrasive in the hand grinder to polish or sand the eye (Fig. 57). Naturally, the wood will clog the stone abrasive, but this doesn't make any difference. You can still polish the groove of the eye with it. All you do is trace over the groove you made with the cutting burr. Do not bear down too hard on the abrasive or linger too long in one place, or you will burn and discolor the wood. These small stone abrasives can be purchased in almost any hardware store. If you use a cheaper version, the stone abrasive is liable to snap off under pressure.

Figure 58 shows how the mouth and tail of the carving in Fig. 55 were carved. After carving, sand with the small sanding drum in the power drill.

Figure 59 is the same carving as in Fig. 53 where the eye is being carved. How to inlay the eye with liquid aluminum is explained in Chapter 4 under the section on the barracuda. This side of the carving was well sanded with a disc cut from a piece of 7/0 garnet paper and then fastened to the Flexbac pad. The carving was then given a coat of Firzite cut 50-50 with benzine, allowed to dry, and then sanded again with 7/0 garnet paper. This time it was sanded by hand. The carving was then given several coats of paste wax. It was polished between each coat with the polishing bonnet in the power drill.

Figure 60 is the opposite side of the carving in Fig. 59. The surface of the

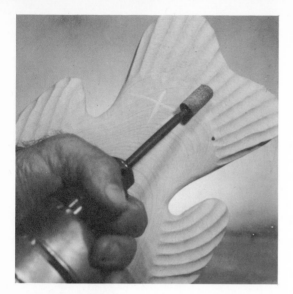

FIG. 56

FIG. 57

FIG. 58

FIG. 59

FIG. 60

carving has been burnished. How this was done and how the body of the fish was carved are described in Chapter 4.

The carving under discussion in this chapter is not a good carving, nor are most of the others; but they do illustrate the procedure and that is all they were intended for. Most have long since been tossed into the fireplace. But there is one carving that has some merit and that is the carving on the top of Fig. 55. This carving is 16 inches long by 9 inches high and 2½ inches thick. What gives this carving an appearance of massiveness is not only its size and thickness, but also the simplicity or, more accurately, the crudeness of the carving. Yet, whatever merit this carving has rests almost solely on the fantastic grain of the wood and on its rich color, a reddish brown.

Project #2

Since these illustrations are fairly clear, comment will be kept to a minimum.

The disc in Fig. 61, when sawed off, will be about 1 inch thick, 8 inches long, and about 7 inches high. It is being sawed off the butt end of a cypress root or knee. Because this wood is so fibrous, you must have power tools, for even with the sharpest chisels or wood gouges it is difficult to work by hand. To get an idea what this wood can be like, imagine trying to carve a ball of cotton. With power tools, however, it is a pleasure.

Notice how vague this sketch is. Even though an ink marker is being used, there is nothing final about it as you will see presently. Never hesitate to change your mind, even after carving has begun. The more flexible you are in this respect, the more original and fresh will be the results. On the other hand, in power-tool carving, you must learn to make up your mind and work quickly once the power has been turned on. Any other sketch than the one illustrated would be as good or

better. Do not follow these sketches, but rather make up your own. Follow only the method of procedure.

The wood marked X (mouth and tail) in Fig. 61 is being removed in Fig. 62.

Figure 63 is a Dumore hand grinder which turns 22,000 rpm, so you don't have to force it. Just touch the wood, and the high-speed rotary file does the rest. In fact, the grinder is so powerful that you have to restrain it rather than force it, or it will carve away more wood than you intended. Because the motor is just above the cutting accessory, the grinder is heavy and somewhat awkward to handle, especially with one hand; but it is a powerhouse, and, once you've adjusted to the weight, most other hand grinders will seem like toys. However, for detail work you must have a lighter grinder. The Dumore illustrated is difficult to control.

Figure 64 shows how to model or shape the body of the fish. Do not bear down on the grinder here, or the cutting tool will dig into the wood. Instead, round the fish's body by just touching the wood you want to remove with the cutting accessory. Push back the fin above the cutter with the wood rasp.

It is important that you observe what is happening in this illustration. It is not the same as in Fig. 63. There you merely traced a groove in the wood over a chalk line. Here you are really carving form with the hand grinder. A light touch is absolutely essential. Try to see the form in your mind; that is, try to visualize how the top of a fish's body gradually curves into the fin, and then shape the wood accordingly. At this stage, don't try to be a perfectionist. It will do if you merely round the fish's body where the rotary file is pointing. Leave the center of the body of your carving more or less flat. Gently curve only the top and bottom. Learning to do what is indicated in the illustration is the one important lesson to absorb in

Fig. 61

Fig. 62

Fig. 63

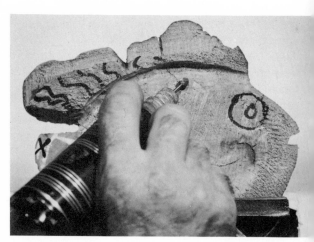

Fig. 64

carving with power tools, for here the cutting accessory is truly an extension of your hand and eye. This may not appear so important now, and in making a fish carving it really isn't; but it will become very important when you begin carving birds, animals, masks, and the human head. For the present, try to get the general idea involved—which is modeling the wood with the cutter—and don't worry too much about what kind of carving results.

Figure 65. Bringing the head and tail to a point with the rasp.

The carving is upside down in Fig. 66, and the lower fin is being sanded. This wood is soft, so you can shape or model it with this gadget. Use a medium sanding disc. Notice how the sandpaper folds over the rubber backing pad. This prevents the sandpaper from digging into the wood. The small rubber back sanding gadget is easier to control than the larger ones. Remember that besides its being able to sand in places where it would be difficult to reach with a larger sanding disc, you can learn to shape or model the wood with this smaller one.

In Fig. 67, the hole is being drilled which will be used later for mounting the piece. This is a mistake; it should have been done after Fig. 62. Never wait until the carving has been brought to a point before drilling this hole, because it is much more difficult then. Since this carving is very light, it was intended to be mounted at the angle pictured; it was thought this might give the carving the appearance of forward motion. The chalk line is a guide for drilling. Notice the gentle curve of the fish's body where it joins the fins. The wood here was modeled with the small sanding disc shown in Fig. 66. This is a good illustration of what can be done with this tool. A good, ¼-inch drill rarely will run hot, so you can take as much time as you need in shaping the wood. Experiment with this power drill. You will soon discover that it can do many things besides straight sanding or drilling holes. You don't have to baby these ¼-inch drills. They were built to take a lot of punishment.

You don't have to baby the hand grinder either, but a hand grinder after prolonged use will run hot. When it does, find something else to do while it is cooling off. The tools in these illustrations have been pushed to their limit, not once, but virtually every time that they were picked up. That they should have stood up to do the work proves they were well made in the first place.

At this point, Fig. 68, it was decided to change the carving to a flounder. The wood marked X above the sketched fins will be removed with a saw. The wood marked xxx on the fish's body will be curved gently where it joins the fin. Here the lower fin is being pushed back further, similar to the top one.

Figure 69 indicates how to model and sand the fish's body with the sanding drum. Notice how the fish's body is beginning to bulge outward.

The small (about 3½ inches) rubber backing pad in Fig. 70 has been cut down from the standard 5-inch size. Use the razor gadget to do this. In cutting down the sanding disc, cut it a little larger so that it will overlap the rubber backing pad. Then fold the edges of the sanding disc back over the pad. This enables you to sand without being fearful that the sanding disc will dig into the wood. You can sand uphill, as it were.

The design is being carved in Fig. 71. After the lower fin is sketched, use a small- or medium-size cutting burr in the hand grinder and trace over your sketch. It is as simple as that. Notice the angry expression on the fish's face. This will be apparent on almost all the fish carvings. The angry look helps to put

Fig. 65

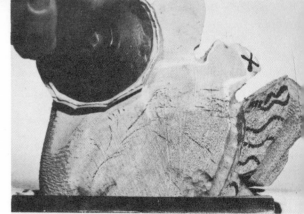

Fig. 66

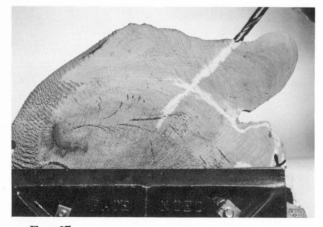

Fig. 67

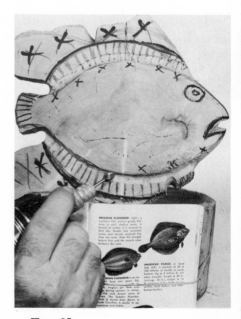

Fig. 68

38

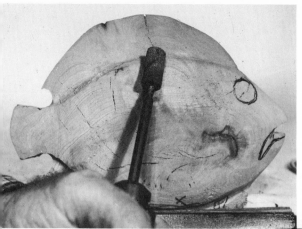

Fɪɢ. 69

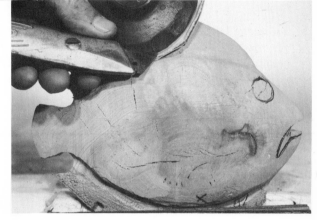

Fɪɢ. 70

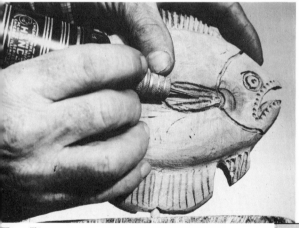

Fɪɢ. 71

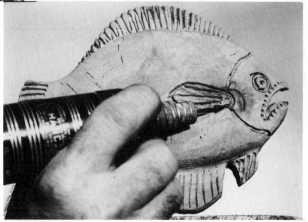

Fɪɢ. 72

some additional life or action in your carvings.

Polishing the grooves in Fig. 72. This carving will be inlaid with aluminum, but should you decide not to inlay your carving, then polish or sand the grooves with a small stone abrasive in the grinder.

Figure 73 demonstrates how to inlay the carving with aluminum. This is an excellent material for inlay work because it dries quickly and is very easy to handle. Do exactly what you see in this illustration.

In a few minutes the aluminum will set. As in Fig. 74, dip your thumb lightly over some wax and press the inlay down hard into the grooves.

Notice the top fin in Fig. 75. Don't try to inlay each individual groove, unless the groove is large; instead spread the aluminum around. The lower fin has already been inlaid.

Remove the surplus inlay (Fig. 76). Use the sanding drum wherever you cannot reach with the sanding disc.

When all the excess inlay has been removed, give your carving a final going over with an 8/0 garnet paper fastened to the Flexbac pad (Fig. 77). Notice the position of the sanding disc. If you were using a regular sanding disc instead of soft garnet paper, the disc would dig into the wood. However, with the garnet paper, you follow the contours of the wood. Actually, since this carving is to be burnished, the final sanding is unnecessary.

Burnishing the carving with a stone abrasive in the ¼-inch drill in Fig. 78. To burnish means to polish or to rub. You can burnish a wood carving by rubbing it with another piece of harder wood. If you wish to burnish with wood and by hand, saw 6 inches off the end of a broom handle or shovel, and rub your carving with the rounded end of the handle. Burnishing presses the wood together and closes the pores. But why do it by hand when you can use the power tool?

These abrasive stones come in many shapes. The one in Fig. 78 is adequate for everything you need. All you have to do is start the drill and rub the spinning stone over the wood. Go over the entire carving —fins, tail, and all. Here you can bear down on the stone as hard as you wish, just so it continues to press the wood and not dig into it. Hold the stone to the wood as is shown.

Figure 79 is the other side of the carving. Notice that it has not been sanded. The lacquer inlay sticks to the rough wood better than if it were sanded. How this inlay is applied is explained in Chapter 10. Here the flame of the torch is applied directly on the lacquer. This causes the colors to blend with one another.

The large flounder on the lower part of the book page is the model in Fig. 80. It required perhaps less than an hour to apply this color. Once the torch is turned on you must learn to work fast. Yet, this side of the carving is much more interesting than the other which required much more work.

Both sides of the finished carving are depicted in Figs. 81 and 82. Again notice the bulge in the fish's body in Fig. 81. Actually, this bulge is less than ½ inch, because the piece of wood to start with was less than 1 inch thick. Remember that it is how you model or shape this bulge in the fish's body that will largely be responsible for what kind of carving results. The face in this carving has not been burnished. It was hoped that this would give the carving contrast, but it is scarcely noticeable. These small carvings make interesting bric-a-brac to have around on shelves or in bookcases. They do not take up much room, and, when you get tired looking at one side, you can turn it around. So you're really getting two carvings in one.

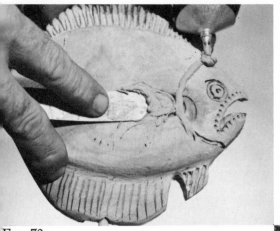

FIG. 73

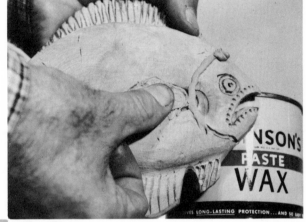

FIG. 74

FIG. 75

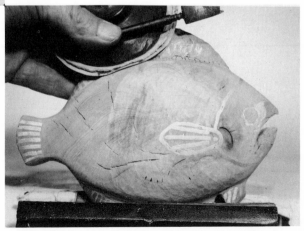

FIG. 76

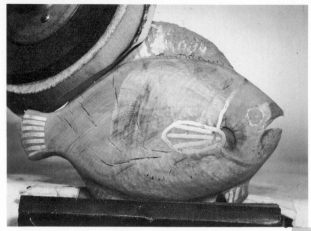

Fig. 77

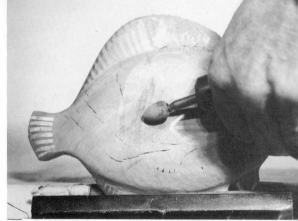

Fig. 78

Fig. 79

Fig. 80

FIG. 81

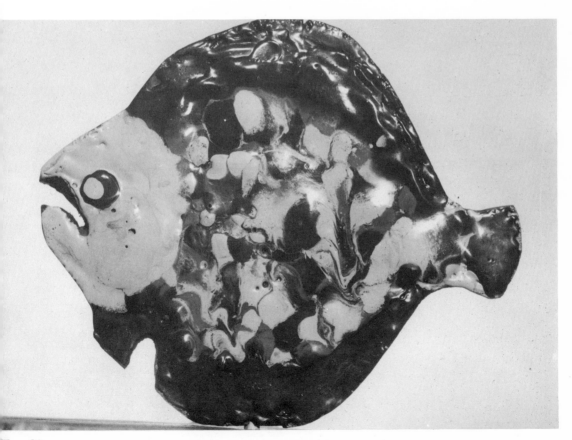

FIG. 82

43

Inlaying with lacquer is fascinating and presents enormous possibilities to anyone with imagination and a willingness to experiment. It is very similar to working with ceramics, except that here you are using the wood for the armature instead of clay. If the fish in Fig. 82 interests you, study ceramics—surface treatment and color—for ideas. All you need to produce a work such as this are a soft piece of wood to use for an armature, some sticks of lacquer, and a torch to melt them. Furthermore, the medium is fairly permanent—work inlaid with lacquer several years ago is still the same today.

Carving with the Grain of the Wood

All previous carvings were made by carving against or into the grain of the wood. The five carvings of fish described in this chapter were not only carved with the grain of the wood, but an attempt was made to make the grain of the wood a part of the carving.

The woods used (scrap lumber) are African mahogany, Peruvian mahogany, Indian teak (two carvings), and Brazilian rosewood. Although the Peruvian mahogany is somewhat harder than the African, both mahoganies and the Indian teak are easy to carve either with hand tools or with power tools. The rosewood is much harder, but still not too hard to work. With the exception of such extremely hard woods as lignum vitae and ebony, it is not too important from a labor standpoint how hard a wood is—most of the carving is done with power tools. But what is important is that a real hardwood not only requires the very best of tools, but it will dull these tools. This applies to the accessories used in the power tools as well as the hand tools.

Any lumberyard dealing in hardwood lumber will have these pieces of scrap around. They are usually the odds and ends of planks that have been trimmed because of cracks, warping, chipping, or other damage. Usually, these pieces are very inexpensive. If you are in doubt concerning how hard or soft a wood is for carving, ask the lumberman. He at least can give you a fair idea. He probably also can tell you anything else you may want to know, such as whether the wood will check or crack once it is carved. Another thing, few lumbermen will sell or even give you a piece of wood for carving unless positive that it is completely dried out.

But what is far more important is the grain of the wood. Try to select a piece that has a grain that will add something to the carving. Unless you start out with such a piece of wood, there is no point in worrying how hard it is or anything else about it. Remember that the grain of the wood is the important thing, and also that it must be there to start with. No matter how skillful a carver you are, you cannot put it there.

If you live in a large city, the chances are that you will not be able to get out in the forest or along a lake to hunt for your own wood. You will have to rely on the nearest hardwood lumberyard or dealer. Try to make certain that the lumber you are using has at least as pronounced a grain as that used in these five carvings. Go through this whole chapter for ideas and suggestions before you begin your carving.

Muskellunge

The muskellunge was carved out of a piece of Brazilian rosewood which measured 20 inches by 4 inches by $1\frac{1}{4}$ inches. This wood is fairly hard to carve with either hand or power tools; yet it is not nearly so hard as lignum vitae or ebony.

First sketch (Fig. 83) to determine how to use the grain of the wood to resemble the scales of the fish.

When it was discovered how hard this piece of wood was, the fins were eliminated, and this meant that the hatchet could be used to remove the surplus wood in the process of rounding the body of the fish (Fig. 84). Notice the short grip on the handle of the hatchet. This makes it easier to control. The hatchet had a razor-thin edge before it was used on this piece of wood. The wood was hard enough to cause the blade to buckle to the extent that it then had to be tempered and sharpened again. When using the hatchet on a hardwood, keep your body well away in case the blade should glance. The face of the fish has been changed from that sketched in Fig. 83 and this is the one that eventually will be carved. The wood around the tail of the fish was removed in sections with the saw. Then the entire carving was worked over with the rasp. A hardwood like this can so dull a rasp that it will have to be replaced. A hole— $\frac{1}{4}$ inch—has been drilled into the fish for mounting in about the center. Do not wait until the carving is completed before you do this; especially is this important if you are bringing the carving to a sharp edge, or if the wood you are using is very thin to begin with. A good policy is to drill this hole for mounting the same size in all your carvings. Then you have only one size dowel pin to bother with, and you also can switch your carvings around from one base to another.

Remove the rasp marks with a medium sanding disc (Fig. 85). The rubber backing pad is the cut-down version. Because the sanding disc overlaps, you can, to some extent, sand in corners—like the inside of the fish's tail. Because it is smaller, this sanding gadget is easier to maneuver than the normal 5-inch size.

The carving, which in Fig. 86 resembles a stranded whale, could be left as is after a thorough sanding. It is not even necessary to carve in the eyes. Sometimes it is best to know when to stop carving, particularly when you are using hardwood. Here, if you are using a hardwood and are leaving your carving simple and without detail, it should be given a very high finish. That is, give it a perfect sanding job and then wax or oil it. The wood in the mouth of the carving was sawed out.

In Figure 87, the lower teeth of the fish carving are being drilled in with the rotary file. Since the wood is hard to begin with, and since you are carving against the grain of the wood, these teeth would have been difficult to carve if you were using hand tools. The teeth in the upper jaw of the fish, because there was ample wood, were drilled in with a $\frac{1}{4}$-inch wood auger in the power drill. These teeth (grooves) will now be sanded with the small sanding drum. Needless to say, it would have been almost out of the question to do this by hand. Yet, with the power tools it was a fairly simple matter.

A small cutting burr is in the hand grinder in Fig. 88. These cutting burrs are inexpensive, and evidently are not made of high-speed steel. In carving with these burrs in a hardwood, do not force them or they will begin to smoke and turn blue, which means that they are burned out and have lost their cutting edge. Three such cutting burrs were used up in doing this small carving. The grooves will be inlaid with aluminum.

The eye in Fig. 89 is being sanded with a tiny sanding abrasive in the grinder.

Compare the view in Fig. 90 with the

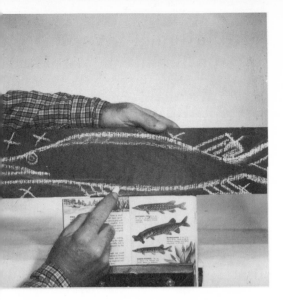

FIG. 83

FIG. 84

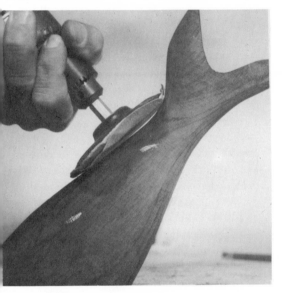

FIG. 85

FIG. 86

FIG. 87

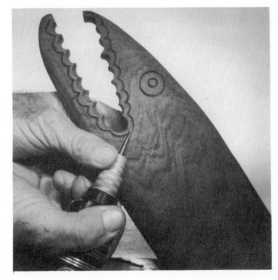

FIG. 88

one in Fig. 86. There will be many occasions when the mere addition of detail not only does not add to the carving but actually may detract from it. This obviously is one such an occasion. Certainly the carving in Fig. 86, even in its unfinished state, is more intriguing.

Sunfish

The sunfish was carved out of African mahogany from a piece 16 inches by 7 inches by ¾ inch. This wood is soft and easy to carve either with hand or power tools.

Figure 91 is the first crude sketch in chalk to determine how best to utilize the grain of the wood.

Once you've decided what to carve, go over the chalk sketch with a black crayon or ink marker to make it more permanent (Fig. 92). Although a sunfish is used as a guide, no attempt will be made to make a realistic copy. Use a saw to remove all surplus wood, except that between the fins and tail which you should drill out with the wood auger in the power drill. Then find the center of balance and drill the hole in the carving for mounting.

This carving will be hung on a wall so it is being carved on one side only. As you can see in Fig. 93, this piece of wood is so soft that you can shape it like a fish merely by pushing the wood gouge with your hands. The wood gouge is razor sharp.

Once you've removed most of the surplus wood with the gouge, go over the carving with the wood rasp (Fig. 94) and then sand with a medium sanding disc. This is not the final sanding, so sand only enough to make it easy to sketch.

Use the small sanding drum (Fig. 95) to sand between the fins and tail, or wherever you cannot reach with the larger sanding discs. Notice how the space between the tail and fins in all these carvings is so carved that you can sand this area of the wood with the sanding drum. This, of course, makes it much easier to sand than if the fin joined the body of the fish at a straight angle. The same applies for the mouth of the fish in most of these carvings. It is just big enough so you can sand it with the sanding drum.

Now carve in the tail, fins, gill, and eyes with the medium cutting burr in the grinder. At first, don't try to cut into the wood too deeply but rather just trace over the sketch lightly. Barely scratch the surface of the wood. Then go back over it again and make the grooves deeper. By following this procedure, you are less likely to make mistakes or have the cutting burr slip off the sketch. It also gives you a last-minute opportunity to change your mind. These grooves will be inlaid with dark mahogany Plastic Wood. If they aren't perfectly spaced or are a bit wobbly, don't worry about it. This suggestion is not made to encourage sloppy craftsmanship, but rather so that you don't get bogged down and upset over some trifling detail. What counts is the whole carving and not some minor detail.

Spread the Plastic Wood over the grooves in the same way you spread peanut butter on a slice of bread (Fig. 96). Then, with a little wax on your thumbs to prevent the Plastic Wood from sticking, press it down hard into the grooves. Allow this to dry for several hours or overnight, and then sand off the surplus with a medium or fine sanding disc. Do not use too coarse a sanding disc or put too much pressure on the power gun, or you will pull the Plastic Wood back out of the grooves. The same applies when sanding off surplus aluminum. The small sanding drum can be used to remove the surplus inlay whenever you cannot do so with the larger sanding discs. To finish, sand with a 7/0 garnet paper and wax.

A carving such as the one in Fig. 97 looks well on a cross section of a log. The

Fig. 89

Fig. 90

Fig. 91

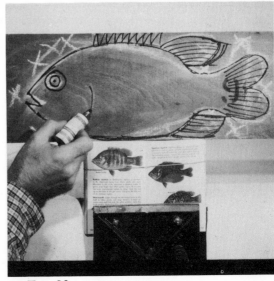

Fig. 92

49

Fig. 93

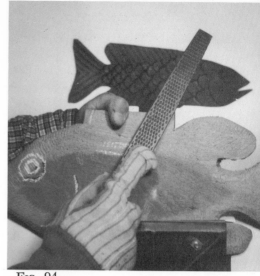

Fig. 94

Fig. 95

Fig. 96

Fig. 97

cross section in this picture is lignum vitae and, of course, is too large. The carving has not been waxed. The reason the grain of the wood is more pronounced is because the floodlights used in taking the pictures strike it at a different angle.

Figure 98 is the finished carving. The base here, too, is lignum vitae. By twisting a small eye hook into one of the top fins, this carving can be hung on a wall.

Flying Fish

The flying fish was carved from a piece of Peruvian mahogany 21 inches by 13 inches by ¾ inch. This wood is slightly harder than African mahogany but still fairly easy to carve with either hand or power tools.

Figure 99 is a piece of scrap lumber purchased from a hardwood lumber dealer. The problem is how to use the sweep of the grain.

The sketch in Fig. 100 is definitely not the answer.

If the tail of the swallow were twisted more to conform to the grain, the sketch in Fig. 101 would make a fair carving.

By altering the swallow sketch slightly, a flying fish is sketched in Fig. 102. Notice how this sketch follows the grain of the wood. The grooving of the wings already has been started. These grooves will later be sanded with the small sanding drum in the power drill. The wood marked *x* between the wings and body of the fish and inside the tail will be drilled out with the wood auger. The rest of the surplus wood can be removed with a saw. As this board is less than an inch thick, it could easily be sawed on a band saw. The entire roughing-out operation would take but a few minutes, since this carving will be left flat and not rounded with the rasp as the other carvings were.

Two ¼-inch holes were drilled into the carving in Fig. 103 for mounting purposes. The other one is where the wing joins the body of the fish. In both places, notice the chalk line which serves as a guide to tell you in what direction to drill. The small pieces of wood that join the ends of the wings to the body were left there to reinforce the wings until the carving was finished. They will be carved away with the rotary file in the grinder once work on the wings is completed. Sanding the wood between the wings and body of the fish and inside the tail presents no problem; the small sanding drum will be used. With the long arbor to which the sanding drum is attached, you can reach almost anywhere.

Carving in the eyes in Fig. 104. Both eyes will be carved alike, but one will be sanded with a small sanding abrasive in the grinder and the other will be filled with walnut Plastic Wood. Remember, do not sand the eye that is to be inlaid with Plastic Wood because the rough edges help to grip the Plastic Wood.

Figures 105 and 106 are two views of the finished carving. The carving has been thoroughly sanded with a sanding disc cut from 7/0 garnet paper and fastened to the Flexbac pad, and then given several coats of wax. The downward thrust of the carving in Fig. 106 is due entirely to the grain of the wood and not the carving. The color of the wood is a rich reddish brown. A simple carving like this looks well if mounted or hung on a wall over a fireplace.

Barracuda

The barracuda was carved from a piece of Indian teakwood 15 inches by 3 inches by 1 inch. This wood is very easy to carve either with hand tools or with power tools. It is so moist and oily that it tends to clog the sanding accessories. Whenever a cutting accessory for the hand grinder becomes clogged with wood, as it will on occasion, clean it with a small wire brush. Naturally you do this when the grinder is not in motion.

Fig. 98

Fig. 99

Fig. 100

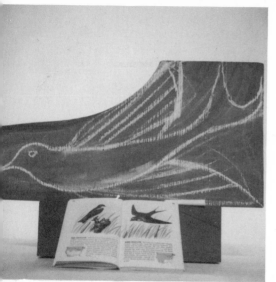

Fɪɢ. 101

Fɪɢ. 102

Fɪɢ. 103

Fɪɢ. 104

Fɪɢ. 105

Fɪɢ. 106

53

Notice in Fig. 107 how only the top portion of this plank, where the grain of the wood is pronounced, is going to be used. All the rest of the wood marked X will be removed with a saw. The body of the fish will then be rounded with the wood gouge, working with the grain—from the head back to the tail in this carving—and then the carving will be rasped with the large wood rasp. This wood is so soft that you can round the body of the fish with the wood gouge without using a mallet. You just push the wood gouge along with your hands. In fact, when using a soft wood like this, you can skip the wood gouge entirely. The coarse wood rasp does the work almost as efficiently, and besides it is easier to control than the gouge.

There are many sanding gadgets on the market but the ones you will probably use most often are the Flexbac pad in Fig. 108 and the small sanding drum in Fig. 109. Notice how the sponge and sanding disc literally fold around the carving. A medium sanding disc is being used. You will seldom have occasion to use anything coarser. The wood in the mouth of the fish will be sawed out.

Use the small sanding drum in Fig. 109 to sand around the fins and the tail where you cannot reach with the larger sanding pad. If the wood you are using is soft, as in this case, you can actually model or shape it by pulling and maneuvering the spinning drum across the surface of the wood. The eyes of the fish will be carved in exactly as sketched.

The side of the carving shown in Fig. 110 will be inlaid with liquid aluminum; the other side will be left plain. A medium-sized cutting burr is being used to carve in the fins and tail.

A wavy line has been grooved around the mouth which is being inlaid with the liquid aluminum (Fig. 111). You spread the aluminum over the grooves the same as you spread toothpaste on a brush. Aluminum dries quickly. In a moment or so it will have set enough so you can press it down hard into the grooves without having too much stick to your fingers. Brushing your thumb lightly over some paste wax will help prevent the aluminum from sticking to you. The aluminum in the eyes and gill has already been pressed down into the grooves. At this stage, don't worry about how messy your carving may look. The important point is to press the aluminum down hard into the grooves. Whatever surplus there is, is easily sanded off once the aluminum has hardened (about an hour or so).

In Figure 112 the fins and tail were inlaid in the same manner as the face. The surplus aluminum was then sanded off with a medium sanding disc. A disc was then cut from a 7/0 garnet paper and fastened to the Flexbac pad, and the inlay and wood given a final sanding. Notice in this picture how the soft garnet paper follows the contour of the wood. This large sanding pad looks awkward to handle, and it is, until you get used to it. However, once you are accustomed to its size and weight, you can do almost any type of sanding with it.

One side of the finished carving is depicted in Fig. 113. The eye was sanded with the small stone abrasive in the grinder. The inside of the mouth was sanded with a table knife wrapped in garnet paper.

The other side of the finished carving is shown in Fig. 114. This carving would look better if the wood below the lower fin were removed and the carving mounted directly on the lower fin. After a thorough sanding with a 7/0 garnet paper, the carving was waxed lightly. It perhaps would look better also if it had not been inlaid in the first place. The base seems about right. A carving like this looks well on a businessman's office desk.

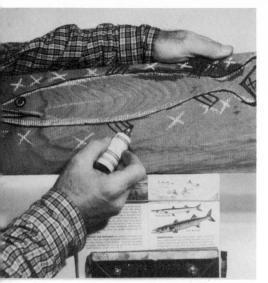

FIG. 107

FIG. 108

FIG. 109

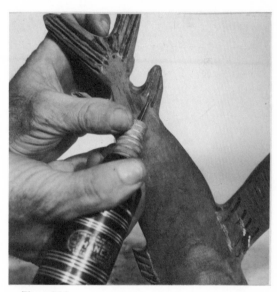

FIG. 110

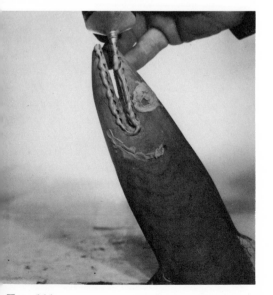

FIG. 111

FIG. 112

FIG. 113

FIG. 114

FIG. 115

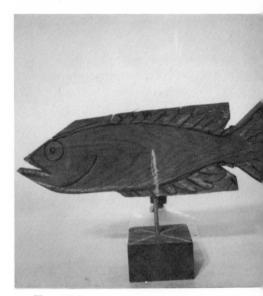

FIG. 116

FIG. 117

FIG. 118

Fig. 119

Fig. 120

Fig. 121

Fig. 122

Largemouth Bass

The largemouth bass was carved from Indian teakwood 15 inches by 5 inches by ¾ inch. This wood is very easy to carve with either hand or power tools.

Notice in Fig. 115 how the grain of the wood is being used to suggest the scales of the fish. This would not be the case if the head of the fish were sketched in where the tail now is.

All roughing out was done with the saw. With the wood rasp, the carving will now be brought to a gradual point both at the head and tail and at the top and bottom. It will then be sanded in order to make sketching easier. Whenever possible, never mount a fish carving as in Fig. 116 with the dowel pin showing. Instead, mount the carving flush to the base.

Since the grain of the wood is not pronounced on this other side of the plank (Fig. 117), scales will be carved. If you find a piece of wood with a pronounced or unusual grain, do not clutter up the carving with surface details, but rather let the grain of the wood speak for itself.

Figure 118 demonstrates how to carve in the fins and tail of the fish with the Foredom flexible-shaft grinder. This is an ideal power tool for a small carving in soft wood. As you can tell, it is very easy to handle—about the same as if you were holding a pencil—so any amount of detail can be carved with it. But in a larger carving, where a lot of wood has to be carved, it lacks the power of the Dumore hand grinder.

Use a small or medium cutting burr to carve in the scales of the fish. The grooves shown in Fig. 119 are about ¼ inch deep.

A high-speed rotary file is in the grinder in Fig. 120. Notice the chalk marks on the edges of the scales. They are a reminder so that you do not carve them off. Instead, you scoop out the wood where the rotary file is pointing. Even though this may look involved, it is really very simple. At least in the beginning, use this chalk guide so that you don't carve away more wood than you intended. The more you make these scales stick out, the more vivid and vigorous will be your carving. You can do this by scooping out the wood in front of the curved edge of the scale at least to the depth of ¼ inch or so. In doing so, you must be careful that you not only don't carve away the edge of the scale on which you are working, but also that you don't cut into the ones directly above it which have already been carved.

One side of the finished carving is shown in Fig. 121. The face, fins, and tail were carved with a small rotary file and then sanded with a small stone abrasive. Then after a thorough sanding, the carving was given a light coat of wax. It would have made a better carving if the fins and tail had been left plain.

This side of the carving, Fig. 122, vaguely resembles an early American wood carving or weather vane. The head has been waxed slightly to bring out contrast with the rest of the carving. You can hang such a carving on the wall or mount it as in this illustration. As you perhaps have noticed, this sort of base fits just about any fish carving. The eye in this carving is inlaid with aluminum.

The Importance of Grain

The simple carving in Fig. 123 illustrates the importance of the grain of the wood but in a different sense. Here the grain does not serve any particular purpose other than to emphasize the beauty of the wood. Since this carving is to be hung on a wall, it is finished on one side only. After using the saw to rough out the carving, it was shaped with the rasp. Except for the carving in the eye and mouth (and this could have been left out), the entire carving was finished with the abrasives in Figs. 124 and 125. Notice the piece of soft wood between the clamp and the carving in Fig. 124. This, of course, protects the carving from damage by the iron clamp.

To finish a simple carving like this, sand thoroughly with a disc of 7/0 garnet paper on the Flexbac pad. Since this is a cross section sawed off the end of a cypress root, you must have power tools—it would be difficult to sand by hand. Now give the carving a coat of Firzite, cut 50-50 with benzine. Allow this to dry overnight; sand again, this time by hand, and wax. The carving is a foot in length (Fig. 126). The color of the wood is a deep reddish brown.

How to Saw a Log in Order to Stretch Out the Grain

The grain of the wood you are using (if it has a pronounced grain) is always important in a carving; but it is especially so in a fish carving. The grain can be used to suggest motion, or it can be used to suggest the scales of the fish. To saw a log to stretch out the grain so that it can be used to suggest the scales of the fish, do the following:

First: Select a small log—the size of a fence post will do—that shows a pronounced grain. You can determine this by how clear the age circles are at the butt end of the log. Then, instead of cutting a disc or slab off the end as in Fig. 127, saw a disc off the log as shown in Fig. 128. The angle is so extreme that you are almost splitting the log lengthwise. Saw this disc about 1½ inches thick. The butt end of the cypress root in Fig. 127 measures 5 inches from top to bottom and slightly more in width. But the disc sawed off in Fig. 129 measures over 12 inches in length. This means that you have stretched the grain to over twice the normal length of the disc in Fig. 127.

The dark part of the wood at which the pencil is pointing in Fig. 130 is the dark center of this root. If this disc were sawed off at the angle in Fig. 127, this dark section would be no more than 1 inch or so in width. Yet here in Fig. 130, it stretches the full length of the disc. The selection of this particular piece of wood was unfortunate because there was little or no grain to start with; yet it does illustrate the method of sawing the log.

Notice later illustrations to see what this

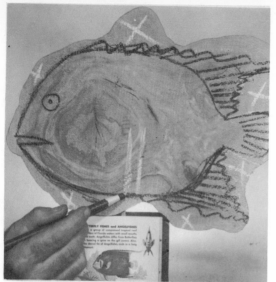

Fig. 123

Fig. 124

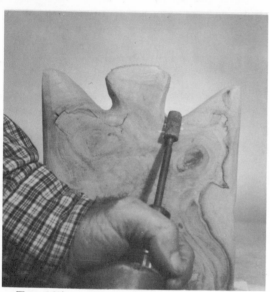

Fig. 125

Fig. 126

Fig. 127

Fig. 128

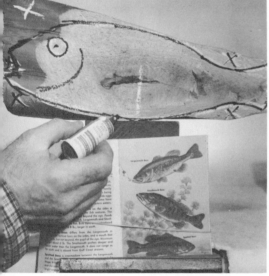

Fig. 129

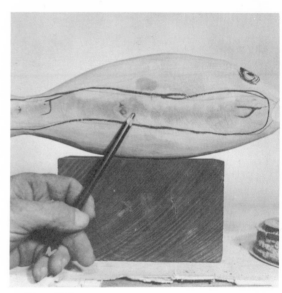

Fig. 130

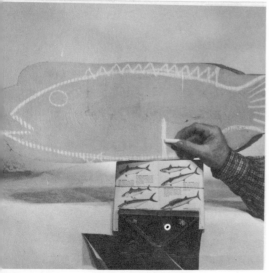

Fig. 131

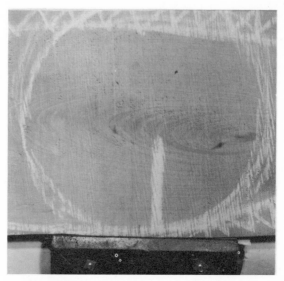

Fig. 132

61

FIG. 133

FIG. 134

FIG. 135

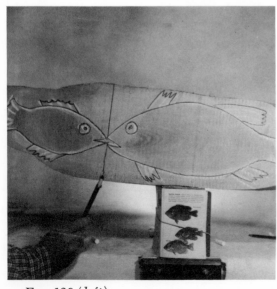

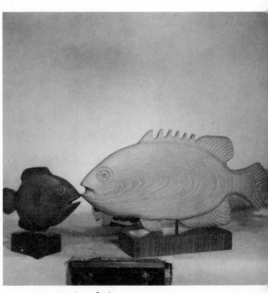

FIG. 136 (*left*)

FIG. 136 (*right*)

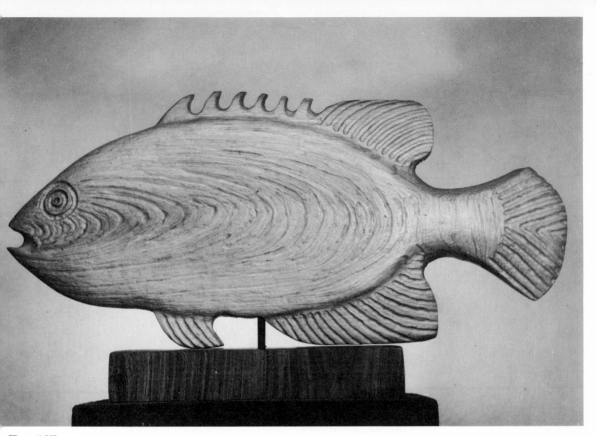

Fig. 137

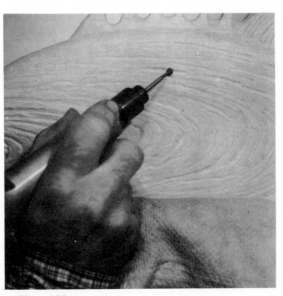

Fig. 138

method of sawing a log can do where there is really a pronounced grain to start with. The discs in the illustrations that follow were sawed from cypress logs and obviously were sawed by machine and not by the author. Since most of these discs are not more than 1 inch thick, and some are no more than ½ inch or ¾ inch, it would be nearly impossible to do this by hand. This wood is very light (the discs weigh little more than an old-fashioned shingle made out of the same wood). It is also very easy to carve.

The cross section in Fig. 131 is 27 inches long by 9 inches high. The heart or center of the log is the dark spot above the knuckles of the hand holding the chalk. This means that the grain of this log has been stretched to three times its normal length because the original size of the log was no greater than the circle drawn in Fig. 132, which is 9 inches across. The chalk sketch in Fig. 131 is all wrong because it does not take advantage of the grain. You might as well be sketching on a plain board.

The fish in Fig. 133, sketched in charcoal over the chalk sketch, shows what is meant by using the grain. Here the fish is reversed so that the grain of the wood resembles scales. The center of the grain of this cross section is where the pencil is pointing, and this will become the eye of the fish.

Figure 134 is the sketch in Fig. 133 completed. The carving is 18 inches long.

Here again in Fig. 135 the large sketch does not take advantage of the wood. The smaller sketch does—the center of the grain is where the charcoal pencil is pointing.

The charcoal line in Fig. 136 (*left*) cuts through the center of the grain, making it possible to make two carvings. In Fig. 136 (*right*) are the finished carvings made from the sketch. Notice how the larger one (18 inches long) departs from the original sketch. This carving, ivory in color, has been given a wax finish. The smaller carving was stained walnut.

The rather unusual finish on the large carving shown in Fig. 137 was made by tracing over the grain with a stone abrasive in the flexible-shaft grinder (Fig. 138). This is the same as burnishing the carving, except that here the grain of the wood is followed carefully. These cross sections were given a light coat of Firzite, cut 50-50 with benzine, to heighten the grain of the wood in order to reproduce it in the illustration. This had the unusual effect of making it possible to bear down hard on the stone abrasive and yet not have it dig into the wood. The stone abrasive in Fig. 138 is pressing the wood, not digging into it or sanding it. The towel in the vise protects the carving from damage.

Carving a Fish in the Round

A large branch of a tree or a small log can be used for this carving (Fig. 139). If the wood you are using is slightly curved or twisted, so much the better; this will give action to your carving. All wood marked X on this carving will be removed with the saw, and then the carving will be rasped.

The finished carving above the sketched one is a fair carving, but it would look better if it were mounted flush to the base. Avoid mounting a carving as this one is mounted. This top carving is about 2½ feet long. Very little about it resembles nature, yet it undoubtedly is a fish.

The carved fish (unfinished) above the sketched one in Fig. 140 is a good example of making a carving the natural way. As you can see in the sketched fish, the form is there before the carving even is begun. After removing the wood marked X in the mouth of the sketched fish with a saw and rasp, you immediately begin carving with the hand grinder. No other roughing out is necessary. By merely tracing over the chalk marks with the high-speed rotary file or cutter, you arrive at the top carving. It is as simple as that. Surely this is more interesting than starting out with a plank, or section of a board. But, you may say, it doesn't really look like a fish. There are hundreds if not thousands of different fish, so how do you know for sure? Both fish forms are about 38 inches long.

A carving like this looks well over the fireplace in a fishing camp or cottage. In fact, since most of the carvings that follow do not have a highly finished appearance, they look best in rustic surroundings, summer homes or cottages, or in the den or bar of a home rather than in the living room.

It doesn't matter what the shape of the wood is you are using. With a little imagination, you can always fit a fish form into it. By just removing the wood marked X in Fig. 141 with a saw, the basic shape of the carving is realized, and ready for the power tools. A hole for mounting has been drilled into the wood where the chalk is pointing.

The large carving in Fig. 142 above the one being carved would look better if hung on a wall. It was carved almost in its entirety with the large cutting burr in the Dumore hand grinder. Whatever merit this carving had is due to the teeth and rough carving.

Use a hatchet to shape the wood to resemble a fish (Fig. 143). This is the most efficient way. Get used to using the hatchet, for entire carvings have been made with it alone.

After using the hatchet, go over the carving with the rasp as demonstrated in Fig. 144.

The wood in the mouth of the fish on the bottom of Fig. 145 was sawed out, and then the jaws of the fish were rasped to give them the slight curve. The grooving

FIG. 139

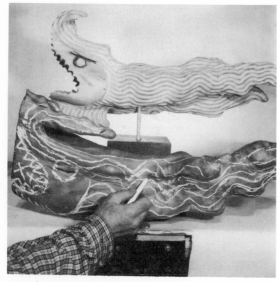

FIG. 140

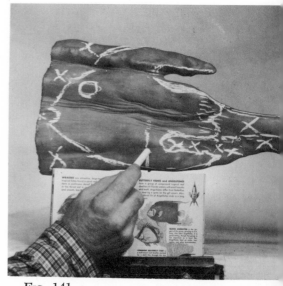

FIG. 141

FIG. 142

FIG. 143

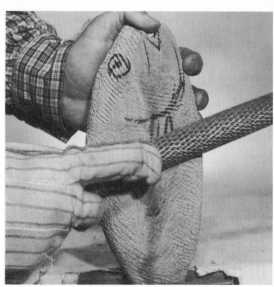

FIG. 144

on the body of the fish is against the grain. Had it been grooved with the grain, as in Fig. 146, it would have made a better carving. To repeat, almost any design you can think up will be better than what you see in these illustrations. The wood for the top carving in Fig. 145 was hollow to start with. The inside of the mouth was first grooved and then sanded with the small sanding drum. Imagine trying to sand this by hand! The hollow part gradually comes to a point 6 or 8 inches inside the cypress knee, so you would be sanding against the grain. But then how would you get your hand on the inside of the knee to sand in the first place? This is especially true where the hollow part comes to a point. Yet, with the sanding drum on the arbor there is nothing to it. You can reach almost anyplace to sand with this gadget. In other words, you must have this sanding gadget to make these carvings.

It does not matter how you curve or twist these grooves; you can still sand them with the gadget shown in Fig. 147.

A fish carving will almost always look better if hung on a wall (Fig. 148). If you have several carvings, arrange them to look like a school of fish.

To mount your fish carving on the wall, twist a small eye hook into it as in Fig. 149. If you want it to hang level, twist the eye hook into it at the center of balance. If you want it to hang on an angle, as those in Fig. 148, move the eye hook slightly forward of the center of balance. These carvings weigh no more than a pound or two, so use the smallest eye hooks you can find. Large ones were used in Fig. 149 in order to make them clearly visible in the illustration. Don't worry about the holes these eye hooks make in your carving. You can always seal them up with a Plastic Wood that matches your carving. To seal up a small hole like this, use a flat toothpick to apply the Plastic Wood.

The grooves on the body of the fish on the bottom of Fig. 150 were sanded with the sanding drum in the power gun. The upper jaw of the carving was grooved against the grain of the wood and then sanded with the small sanding drum as in Fig. 151. The lower jaw in the carving in Fig. 150 was grooved with the grain of the wood and then sanded. The eye was carved exactly as you see the eye being carved in Fig. 152. Just carve away the rest of the *xxxx*'s around the eye in this picture, and you are ready to sand it.

Study carefully the three fish on top of the one that is being carved (Fig. 150). It involves no more work to make a fish carving out of a twisted or curved piece of wood than it does to make one out of a straight one. Yet notice how much more fascinating any of these carvings are because of the twist of their bodies. How to put action or movement in your carvings is discussed in Chapter 6. Many, if not most, fish exist by eating each other. Once you have completed a half-dozen or more fish carvings, interesting wall murals in wood can be worked out. The wood (cypress) is very light in weight, so hanging these fish carvings on the wall presents no problem. The smaller fishes in this group are only wedged into the mouths of the larger. This group of fish carvings, if mounted over a fireplace in a sportsman's den, would definitely add something to the room. Yet all it takes to make them are a few small cross sections and a few twisted branches of wood.

The carving at the bottom of Fig. 153 is finished as far as carving is concerned, but it has not been waxed; plainly, it is not worth the wax. The carving on the face of the fish was done with a small cutting burr in the small grinder and is entirely unnecessary—it adds little or nothing to the carving. The grooving on the body of the fish is all wrong. In short, this carving is clearly destined for the fireplace, where

FIG. 145

FIG. 146

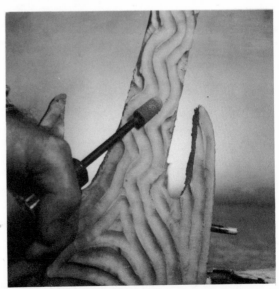

FIG. 147

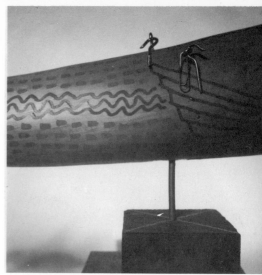

FIG. 148

FIG. 149

FIG. 150

FIG. 151

FIG. 152

FIG. 153

F𝙸𝙶. 154

F𝙸𝙶. 155

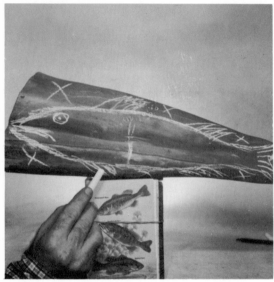

F𝙸𝙶. 156

F𝙸𝙶. 157

F𝙸𝙶. 158

FIG. 159

FIG. 160

FIG. 161

FIG. 162

FIG. 163

it belongs. Yet, it does suggest some sort of fish and that is all it was intended to do. The eye in this carving was not only sanded but actually shaped with the sanding drum you see in Fig. 154. The scales of the fish directly above the one that is being carved in Fig. 153 were first grooved with the small rotary file in the grinder in Fig. 155, and then sanded with a small stone abrasive in the same grinder.

Movement and Action

It requires very little extra work to make a carving of a fish out of a twisted branch of a tree than to make it out of a straight piece of wood. Yet notice how much more interesting such a carving is. You will find such pieces of wood usually along a lake shore or river bottom, and when you do, collect them for later use. If you were using only hand tools, these twisted forms, because they are mostly full of knots, would add a lot of extra work. It is also often difficult to work with the grain of a twisted piece of wood with hand tools. But with power tools all this doesn't matter. You can reach almost anywhere to carve with a hand grinder; and the same applies to the ¼-inch drill when used for sanding.

Figure 156 is not an appealing sketch and if finished as is would not be worth the labor involved.

Actually, Fig. 157 isn't much better than Fig. 156; but it does convey (by the slight arch in the fish's body) the impression of a fish leaping out of water. To carry out that idea, this carving could be mounted, when completed, by drilling a hole up into the tail of the fish.

If you are using a straight piece of wood that allows no room for twisting the fish's body, you can still put some action into your carving by emphasizing the teeth or the face as in Fig. 158.

The wood between the tail and the body in Fig. 159 was drilled out with the wood auger in the ¼-inch drill. After rasping, it was sanded with the small sanding drum in the same drill.

Whatever merit the unfinished carving in Fig. 160 may have is due to the twist of the wood, and this was there before the carving was begun.

This carving, Fig. 161, was left in its rough state; that is, no effort was made with abrasives to remove the tool marks.

The carving in Figs. 162 and 163, about a foot in length, although made from a twisted piece of cypress root, could just as well have been carved from a curved piece of driftwood. Naturally, this isn't the correct base for such a small carving, but notice the impression of movement in the mountings. Never hesitate to experiment in mounting your fish carvings in unconventional ways. Don't worry about drilling extra holes in your carving; these can always be plugged up with a wooden dowel pin and then sealed with some Plastic Wood that matches the wood. You can learn to do this so skillfully that it is almost impossible to tell where the hole was drilled. Also, should a portion of your carving crack or break off (it is difficult to imagine how this can happen in a fish carving), don't let it upset you. There are glues or cements on the market so efficient that they strengthen the carving once you've glued the broken pieces together again. This can also be done so skillfully that you almost won't be able to tell where the pieces are joined.

Carving Birds

Project #1

To get started carving bird forms, begin with an easy project like the following. Either one or both of these carvings can be made in a single evening.

For Fig. 164, the wood is African mahogany and measures 12 inches by 7 inches by 1 inch. Divide the board as in the illustration. Of course, you don't have to use this particular wood nor does it have to be this size. Any piece of scrap lumber such as maple, walnut, teak, or oak will do. But use hardwood lumber and not soft. Now sketch in a bird form in each half—a duck or any other bird. Have the bird looking backward or preening itself, if you wish. Whatever you sketch, try to fill the wood. All wood marked X in these sketches will be removed. Do not try to carve in the legs of a bird—they will only snap off. Although a snipe is pictured in the book below the sketch, no attempt has been made to copy it. It will be enough if your carving can be identified as a bird; never mind what kind. Use the pictures in the book only as a guide.

A bird is being roughed out in Fig. 165. A saw was used wherever possible. The wood behind the bird's head was drilled out with the wood auger in the $\frac{1}{4}$-inch drill. All that holds these birds together are the 2 inches or so of wood on the back of the lower bird. To separate them, merely make the groove deeper with the hand

grinder and break them apart. Only one side of these birds will be carved, so only one side will be rounded with the rasp. The other side will be left as is and inlaid with melted lacquer. If you do not care to experiment with color, leave the other side uncarved anyway; a carving like this looks best on a wall. A large high-speed rotary file is in the hand grinder. You have only to guide the grinder over the sketch; electricity does the work. For a carving like this, do not use a hardwood; not because the hand grinder can't carve it, but because a hardwood dulls the rotary file the same as it dulls any other tool. Furthermore, these small carvings aren't worth carving in a hardwood.

Figure 166 shows the sanding of the grooves. Notice how sharp the edges of the sanded grooves are in contrast to those that are unsanded.

After rasping with the wood rasp, go over the carving with the rubber back sanding pad shown in Fig. 169. Wherever you cannot reach with the sanding gadget, use the sanding drum as shown in Fig. 167. The eye and the bill were carved in as in Fig. 168, and then sanded with a small stone abrasive in the same hand grinder. Notice the tuft on the back of this and the other bird's head. These were not in the original sketch and are the result of the way the wood was drilled in Fig. 165.

The eye is being carved in Fig. 168. This eye will be inlaid with dark mahog-

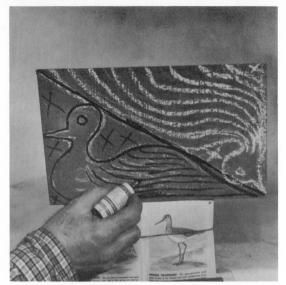

FIG. 164

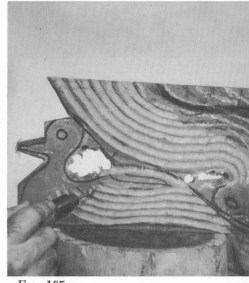

FIG. 165

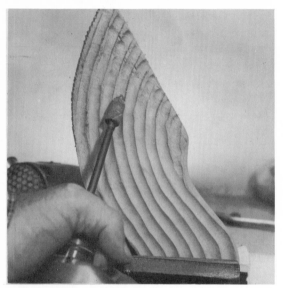

FIG. 166

FIG. 167

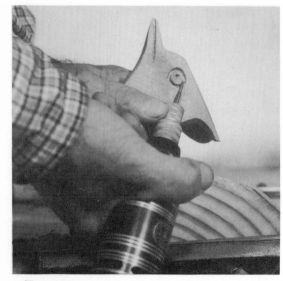

FIG. 168

FIG. 169

FIG. 170

FIG. 171

FIG. 172

FIG. 173

FIG. 174

FIG. 175

any Plastic Wood, so it will be left rough. The rough edges help to grip the Plastic Wood.

After pressing the Plastic Wood down hard into the eye and bill, allow it to dry for an hour or so and then sand off the surplus (Fig. 169). While you're waiting for the Plastic Wood to dry, you can work on the other carving. The rubber back sanding pad is the cut-down one already discussed.

To make the holes in Fig. 170, you have only to touch the wood with the medium-sized cutting burr—the hand grinder does the rest. Dark mahogany Plastic Wood will be spread over these holes with the spatula and then pressed down hard with the thumb. After it is dry, the surplus will be sanded off.

The wooden dowel pin in Fig. 171—barely visible because it is painted a flat black—is slightly forward of the center of the carving. If it were an inch or two longer it would look better. A good guide is to make these dowel pins about the actual length of a bird's leg. Also, drill the hole into the carving at approximately the same place where the bird's legs are joined to its body. Brass or bronze dowel pins look better than wooden ones. This is not the right base. A good base for this type of carving is a 1-inch-thick disc sawed off a small tree or branch. Leave the bark on the disc and do not sand the top, but rather leave it rough. Let your common sense tell you how large around the base should be. (See Chapter 12, "Bases.")

Figure 172—one side of finished carvings. Making a carving from a flat board or a block of wood is not as interesting as one you carve from a piece of wood—driftwood, cypress knee, etc.—where the basic shape of the carving is already there.

The colors on the other side of this carving (Fig. 173) are the colors of a blue jay—blue, black, and white. Notice how the surface of the wood on this carving and on the one in Fig. 174 has been scratched with the cutting burr in the hand grinder in order to help the melted lacquer take hold. To apply the lacquer, you hold the stick to the flame of the torch until you notice it beginning to melt and then quickly spread it on the carving. You must work fast, because the lacquer dries almost instantly. As you can well imagine, the color is rather difficult to control, so do not try for an exact copy of whatever you might be coloring. A vague impression will do.

In Fig. 174, you just melt the colors and let them drip on the wood. First apply one color all over the carving, and then do the same with another, etc. The colors on this carving are green, black, and white, but mostly green. After the wood has been fairly well covered with the drips of the colors, the flame of the torch will be held directly on the colors. This causes the colors virtually to come alive and to blend with each other. It is a fascinating process to watch, and, with practice, some startling results can be achieved.

Figure 175 shows the other side of the finished carvings. The tube leaning against the carving is Plastic Porcelain. You apply the liquid porcelain directly from the tube. Whether this Plastic Porcelain would adhere to the wood if applied directly from the tube is unknown. More than likely it will not, because what makes the melted lacquer stick is the fact that it literally is burned into the wood. But surely this Plastic Porcelain will adhere to lacquer already on the wood, and can be used to touch up a carving already inlaid with lacquer. Small amounts (the small white dots) were applied to the carving in the foreground by just touching the tube to the carving. The flame of the torch was then applied directly to the top half of the carving to see if the Plastic Porcelain would blend with the lacquer.

As you can see it does. The color of this Plastic Porcelain is a shade whiter than the white lacquer. There are many such new products on the market. Experiment with them. You might be surprised at the results.

A Bird Form in the Round

As already mentioned, a carving in the round is not only carved on all sides, but so carved that it looks right from any position. What this means to you as a carver, is that you should be certain that the form you intend to carve can be fitted into the piece of wood you are using. The best way to do this is to take a piece of chalk and sketch the form directly on the wood. This sketching does not have to be accurate in the sense that you have to make a good drawing. The author scarcely can draw a straight line. You do this sketching only to get a rough idea of whether the project you have in mind is practical in relation to the wood you are using. It does not matter how crude this sketch is —it is intended only as a rough guide. Study the sketches that accompany these chapters on carving and you will get a good idea of how to proceed.

The bird form 23 inches high in the center of Fig. 176 is a good example of what is meant by co-operating with what nature has already put there. Remove all the wood marked X with a saw and hatchet; go over the sharp edges with a wood rasp and you practically have the finished carving. All you would have to do to complete the job is to sand the carving with a sanding disc in the ¼-inch drill, carve in the bill and eyes with a small cutting burr in the hand grinder, and, if you like, give it a coat or two of wax. The entire project shouldn't involve more than a few hours' work, and, since most of this work is done with power tools, it's really no work at all. Obviously, the other two carvings pictured were made from a similiar-shaped piece of wood. The bird form on the right is inlaid with pure lacquer color mixed with Plastic Wood. The Golden Nature Series pocket book is entirely adequate as a guide. Use this book only as a reference to discover where to carve in the eye of the bird, where the wings join the body, etc. If you will keep this in mind you won't get bogged down in meaningless detail. A small tree that comes to a fork, or a large branch that does the same, can be used to make these carvings, especially the small carving on the left. A piece of driftwood would be even better because usually you don't have to remove the bark before sketching.

Figure 177 is about the same as the sketch in Fig. 176, except that it would be even easier to make. The entire upper part of this carving could be made with a wood rasp, and the wood where the hand is could be sawed out. The fact that legs are sketched in does not mean that they will be carved. Never do this where you are working against the grain of the wood, as you would be in this instance. It not only involves a lot of work, but the legs snap off at the slightest bump. Generally, in a carving like this, it is enough if you sketch only one side. Now turn the carving so that it is facing you, and, with your eyes, estimate if the depth of the wood is sufficient. If it is, go over the sketch with an ink marker to make it more permanent and start carving. You don't have to do any more sketching either in the front or back or on the other side.

There is no point in making the same carving over and over, so turn this piece of wood around, lay it on its side, and sketch in a rabbit form (Fig. 178). For all its crudeness, this rabbit sketch, if carved exactly as it is, would make the most interesting carving in the book. The fact that there isn't enough wood to carve in both hind legs of the rabbit doesn't matter. It would still make a good carving of a running rabbit. The *X* chalk mark on the rabbit's body was put there only to help focus the camera while taking the picture. Wherever these *X*'s or other markings appear inside the outline of a sketch or carving, they were usually put there for the same reason.

The finished carving on the right in Fig. 179 could have been fitted into this piece of wood, but the sketched one—a rooster drinking water—would make a better carving. This piece of wood looked at from the bottom resembles a triangle. This also is a very easy carving to make.

Notice particularly in the bird carvings that follow how an attempt was made to give them some action by making it appear as if the bird form were doing something—the head is turned, the neck is twisted or stretched, the body is turned, or the bill of the bird is open. Any of these things will help to put life into your carving.

In Fig. 180, notice how the carving in the front departs slightly from the original sketch in Fig. 176. A base has been substituted for the legs, which is right, but the mouth of the bird is closed, which is a mistake. An open mouth tends to give action to a carving. The saw was used to saw a V-shaped wedge out of the front of the carving to form the lower part of the breast and base. But the hatchet and the coarse rasp were used to remove the rest of the wood marked *X* in Fig. 176. The hatchet, tempered and with a razor-sharp edge, can be dangerous both to yourself and the carving if not handled carefully. Take a short grip on the handle and use it the same as a butcher uses a meat cleaver on the butcher's block. Part of the head and neck have already been rasped, but the hatchet marks are still visible on the breast. The grooving for the wings and tail is done exactly as shown in Fig. 181. You merely trace over the design you have sketched with the high-speed rotary file,

and the electricity does the rest. Notice how these grooves are spaced.

The breast and the base of the bird form in the background of Fig. 180 were inlaid with melted lacquer, porcelain, shellac, and marble. The colors were melted with a small torch and allowed to drip on the wood in the same manner as in Fig. 182.

The wood behind the head of the rooster in Fig. 181 was drilled out with a $\frac{3}{8}$-inch wood auger in the $\frac{1}{4}$-inch drill. What wood is left can be knocked out with a chisel or wood gouge. You don't have to buy a regular wood mallet for this, because you are not going to use a gouge or chisel that much. Instead, saw a foot or so off the top of a baseball bat. If the bat is fairly heavy, this will make an excellent mallet. The wood in the mouth of the rooster will be carved out with the same accessory shown. The rotary file is carving directly against the grain of the wood, as naturally the grain runs from the base upward. While it isn't too important, it would have been easier to have made these grooves starting from the base of the carving and working upward. Even with power tools, it is always better and more sensible to work with the grain of the wood.

If the wood you are using is soft, then do your rasping with the coarsest wood rasp you can find, as in Fig. 183.

The entire carving in the center of Fig. 184 has been gone over with the sanding disc in the $\frac{1}{4}$-inch drill, using a medium sanding disc. The grooves in the wings were sanded with the sanding drum, the same as the grooves are being sanded in Fig. 185. Compare the wing with the tail, and notice how the thin edge of wood between the grooves has been brought to a sharp point in the wings. The sharper these edges are, the better the carving. It gives it a crisp, neat look. It may appear difficult to sand these grooves, not only

Fig. 176

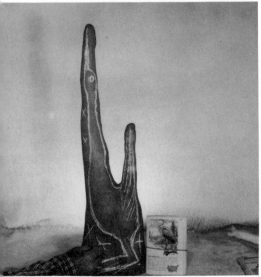

Fig. 177

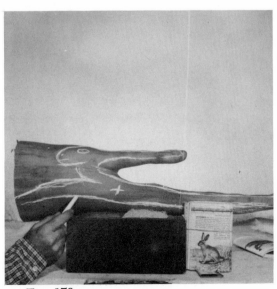

Fig. 178

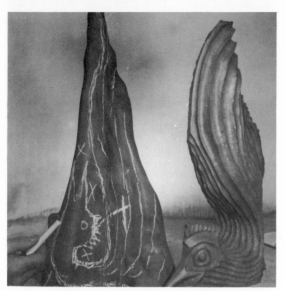

FIG. 179

FIG. 180

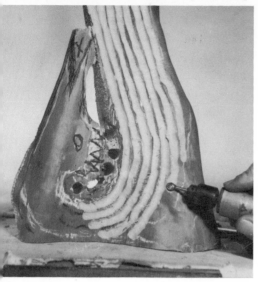

F<small>IG</small>. 181

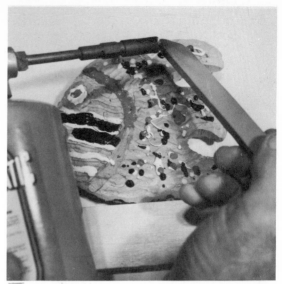

F<small>IG</small>. 182

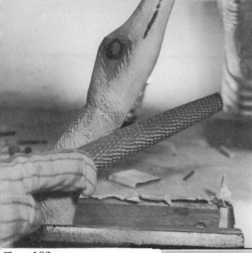

F<small>IG</small>. 183

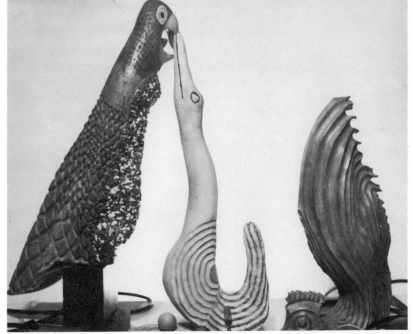

F<small>IG</small>. 184

around corners but also against the grain of the wood, and it would be if you were doing it by hand. However, with the drill and the sanding drum it is a simple matter. Remember not to force the sanding drum or to bear down on it. Just guide it along the grooves and let the electricity do the work.

The side of the rooster to the right in Fig. 184 was finished almost entirely with this little sanding drum, except the wider grooves which were sanded with the ½-inch abrasive arbor in Fig. 186. These abrasive arbors come in three sizes—¼ inch, ½ inch, and 1 inch. The parrot to the left in Fig. 184 represents a great deal of wasted time and effort. If the wood you are using is not the right piece for what you are carving or intend to carve, nothing you do can turn it into a good carving. This was such a case. The wood was simply not suited for a parrot carving. Yet something else might have been carved out of it. Naturally, the base is too small.

In Fig. 185, the sanding drum is being used against the grain of the wood. It would have been much easier to sand if the carving had been turned around. The wood between the head and body has been rasped. The same sanding drum will be used to sand this area.

Figure 187 explains itself. The small wooden ball on the base of the carving was not carved by the author but was purchased in a woodworking shop. The basic shape of the carving of the angry hen in the background was there before work was begun. The wood was cut in a cypress swamp in southern Louisiana. Except for the grooving and the coloring done by the author, this is exactly the way it grew.

Notice how the carving is mounted in Fig. 188. If it were mounted in the center of the base, it would look off balance. Originally two holes were drilled into the base of this carving and metal dowel pins inserted to resemble the legs of the angry hen. Only seldom will an arrangement like that benefit your carving, and it is best to mount it flat or flush to the base. The base in this carving is reddish African mahogany. A single wooden dowel pin is enough to hold the carving to the base. The color of the cypress in this picture is yellowish-ivory. It was a mistake to add the color to this beautiful piece of wood.

The finished carving is in the center of Fig. 189. A small cutting burr in the small hand grinder was used to carve in the eyes and bill. The best way to do this is to trace over the sketched eye and bill (see Fig. 187) very lightly with the small cutting burr. Then put a medium-sized burr in the hand grinder and go over it again, making the groove deeper and wider. By following this procedure, you are less likely to make a mistake. Now with a small stone abrasive, sand the eye and bill as in Fig. 190. This is not a good carving, but it is an easy one to make and will do for a first attempt at making a bird carving. What is wrong with the carving? Almost everything. The head and neck are too big in relation to the body of the bird. Then there is too much grooving. Had the grooving been stopped at the stage in Fig. 184, it would have helped some. The base should not have been grooved at all. In fact, if the carving were sawed off the base and mounted on another of different wood, it would help.

The angry goose in the background, even in its unfinished state, is superior. After carving in the face of the goose, the whole thing should be burnished with the large abrasive stone in the ¼-inch drill. No grooving or any other carving will be done. The carving is about life-size.

The rooster on the right is the opposite side of the rooster in Fig. 184. It was carved with the large cutting burr in the Dumore hand grinder is pictured in Fig. 191. As you can see, no attempt has been made to sand this side. The appearance

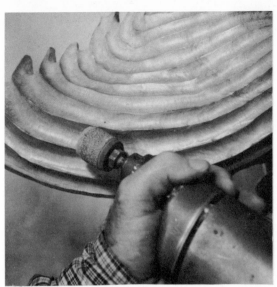

Fig. 185

Fig. 186

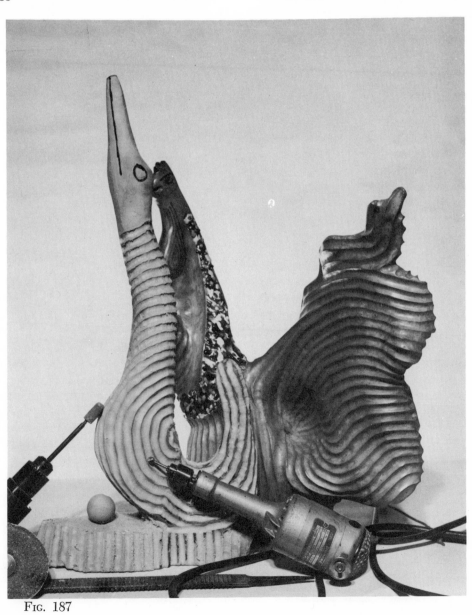

Fig. 187

F<small>IG.</small> 188

F<small>IG.</small> 189

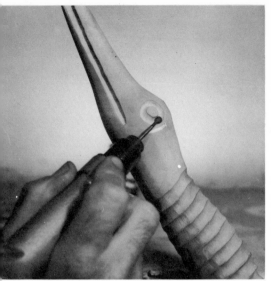

Fig. 190

Fig. 191

Fig. 192

of a carving can sometimes be improved by waxing, but this rooster is simply not worth it. If your carving does not turn out as you had hoped, never throw it away or destroy it; you can always carve something else out of it. It would take but a few minutes to remove the grooves in the rooster with a wood rasp. As a last resort, you can always make a fish carving out of it. A lamp could be made out of this carving (and many of the others that follow) by drilling a hole down through the center of the back and base of the bird, and inserting a metal tube for the wiring and for holding the lamp socket and shade.

Owl

The wood on which the sketch is made in Fig. 192 is an 18-inch section of a cypress knee or root. It is 5 inches across the top. Except for the excess wood marked X around the legs of the owl and on the top of the head, there is very little roughing-out work to do. The head and body of the owl completely fill the rest of the wood. For a carving like this, use a dried-out section of a log or fence post. The body and the head of an owl are more or less round. Using a round log means that this much of your carving is already completed before you ever touch the wood. There are no sharp corners or edges to carve away which would be necessary if you were using a block of wood. The legs of an owl seldom are visible when it is perched on a branch, so it is entirely unnecessary to carve them. In fact, it is unlikely that an owl would stand in this position. If you decide not to carve in the legs, then a 10- or 12-inch section of a log should do. The hand grinder and the accessory show how the holes were carved into the body and head of the finished young owl. Figure 193 shows how these holes were polished or sanded with the stone abrasive in the small grinder.

Of the three sketched owls (Figs. 194,

195, and 196), the one in Fig. 196 is the most interesting. It would also be the easiest carving to make. Keep your sketch and carving as simple as possible The horns or tufts in the sketch in Fig. 196 are unnecessary Mostly, an owl carving will be more intriguing if the owl is looking over its shoulder.

The saw was first used to shape the tufts or horns of the owl on the left in Fig. 197 as well as to remove the wood around the bottom. The top of the owl's head was then rounded with the wood rasp. Carving of the face and wing already has been started with the hand grinder. The grooves are between $\frac{1}{4}$ and $\frac{1}{2}$ an inch deep. The saw is by all odds the most efficient tool there is for roughing out your carving. In this case, the wood around the bottom of the owl had to be removed. Except for the bill of the finished owl on the right, at no other place does the carving penetrate the wood more than $\frac{1}{2}$ or 1 inch. In other words, this piece of wood is still almost perfectly round. Yet, because of the surface treatment, it does suggest an owl. Whenever possible, avoid mounting a carving done in the manner of the finished owl. If you can't think of any other way, hang it on a wall as in Fig. 198.

Figure 199 is a good illustration of how to block out a carving with the saw. At this stage, only the saw has been used; yet the basic shape of the owl already is realized. As mentioned earlier, it is unnecessary to carve in the legs of the owl. Instead, do as in this illustration and carve in only the feet. The finger is pointing at the feet of the owl where a $\frac{3}{8}$-inch hole has been drilled in order to mount the carving. A $\frac{1}{4}$-inch hole would have been adequate. The tail behind the hand is much too long for an owl carving. This is the back view of the owl.

Figure 200 shows the rasping of the owl. All that has been done is to rasp the sharp edges left by the saw in Fig. 199. This is

FIG. 193

FIG. 194

FIG. 195

FIG. 196

F<small>IG</small>. 197

F<small>IG</small>. 198

F<small>IG</small>. 199

actually the back of the owl's head. The sketching and carving have been done only to show that you don't have to reproduce the face of an owl exactly true to nature. A design similar to this will be fine. In all probability an owl carving finished along these lines would make a better piece than if you tried to make an accurate copy.

Figure 201 is the face of the owl. If the face of the owl in some of the other illustrations strikes you as difficult or involved, carve in a simple face as demonstrated here.

The wings of the owl on the left in Fig. 202 project out from the body ½ inch at most. The wood on the breast between the wings either can be carved away with the rotary file in the hand grinder or, as in this case, carved away with the wood gouge and mallet. The wood between the legs was ground out with the rotary file, and the lower part of the body and the legs have been rounded with the rasp.

Figure 203 shows how the upper part of the wings was carved. Use the small or medium cutting burr.

Figure 204 shows how the lower part of the wings was carved. To carve the wings as in Fig. 202, make the two outside grooves in the wing first, and then work into the center.

There is nothing true to nature in the finished owl in Fig. 202, except maybe the bill. Yet it looks like an owl. This carving can also be hung on a wall or better still mounted on a cross section of a log of appropriate size. Your own common sense is a safe guide in regard to what size to make this base. How to mount a carving such as this is explained in Chapter 12, "Bases."

The simulated feathers on the breast of the finished owl in Fig. 202 were grooved in with a small rotary file and then polished with a stone abrasive. The edges of these feathers were then carved with a small cutting burr as in Fig. 205. Note the position of the cutting burr as it is touched to the wood. This carving was thoroughly waxed.

Aside from the carving on the head of the owl on the right in Fig. 206, the main difference between this and the left-hand carving in Fig. 202 is that the entire carving has been worked over with the sanding disc shown in Fig. 207. The grooving in the top part of the wings has been widened with a small rotary file as shown in Fig. 208. These grooves were then sanded with a small stone abrasive in the same grinder. The face of the owl was carved with the large rotary file. The V form (bill) on the face of the owl, along with the upper part of the wings, will be sanded and waxed to bring out contrast with the rest of the carving which will be left rough. The owl on the left was carved almost entirely with the cutting burr in the grinder in Fig 209. Again, the V shape on the face of the owl and the eyes were sanded and waxed to bring out contrast with the rest of the carving which is left in the rough.

Figure 210 shows another way to carve in the upper part of the wings. The eyes in this picture are very easy to carve. Naturally, the deeper you carve the large outside circle, the more the eye of the owl will project.

Figure 211 is the finished owl. Only a small opening has been made between the legs of the owl. To mount this carving, drill a ¼-inch hole about an inch deep up into the feet of the owl and use a wooden dowel pin to fasten it to the base. A 2- or 3-inch-thick cross section of a log will make an excellent base. This base should be no bigger around than is necessary to prevent the carving from toppling over. Leave the bark on the base.

Figure 212 shows how the legs, body, and back of the head of the owl were carved. A medium cutting burr is in the

FIG. 200

FIG. 201

FIG. 202

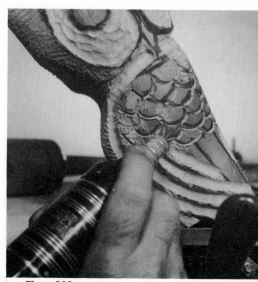

FIG. 203

Fig. 204

Fig. 205

Fig. 206

Fig. 207

Fig. 208

Fig. 209

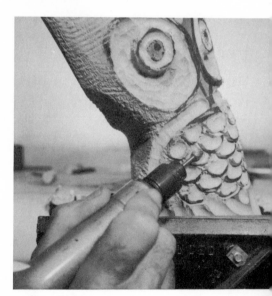

Fig. 210

Fig. 211

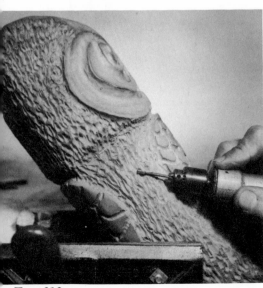

Fig. 212

Fig. 213

grinder. All you do is scratch the surface of the wood with the burr as indicated.

Figure 213 shows how the face of the owl was sanded. With a little practice, you can learn to do almost anything with the small sanding drum.

Figure 214 shows how the lower part of the wings and the feet of the owl were sanded. Notice that the sanding drum in this picture gradually has been worn to a point. This is not the same sanding drum as in Fig. 213. You can make at least six such carvings as this one before the sanding drum will wear down to this extent. The worn-down one was used here in order to sand the grooves.

Figure 215 is the finished carving. Both this owl or the one in Fig. 211 are fair carvings and would make excellent decorations for a summer home or cottage or fishing camp. Exhibit them the same as you would exhibit an owl mounted by a taxidermist. Naturally, a carving is much easier to clean or dust than a mounted specimen.

Duck

Making a carving of a duck is no more difficult than the owl. The only difference is that here you are going to try to make the piece of wood you are using resemble a duck—any duck.

Carving a duck (Fig. 216). The natural way to carve a duck is to select a piece of wood that already vaguely suggests a duck, or a piece of wood into which the outlines of a duck can be fitted easily without having to remove too much surplus wood. The piece of wood in the illustration—a cypress root or knee looked at from the front or the base—somewhat resembles a pyramid or triangle. The head of the duck is sketched in to fill the top of this pyramid and the breast and body fill in the base. The chalk sketch is only a rough outline to indicate what wood to remove in the roughing-out process. Take advantage of all the wood in making the sketch, especially any odd shape it may have. There is nothing final about this sketch. If you don't like it or if it doesn't take full advantage of the shape of your wood, wipe it off with a damp cloth and start over again. In the sketch, the duck could just as well have been looking backward or preening itself. There is sufficient wood, and it would have made the carving more interesting. This twisting of the head or body of your carvings is important—it gives them movement and action.

Obviously the same piece of wood is being sketched in Figs. 217, 218, and 219. Figure 217 is a pigeon preening itself, Fig. 218 is a sleeping duck, and Fig. 219 is also a duck. Of the three, the pigeon would make the best carving. The wood between the head and body of the bird could be drilled out with a wood auger in the $\frac{1}{4}$-inch drill. The duck in Fig. 219, the least interesting, will be carved.

The inlaid duck in Fig. 216 was a fair carving before it was inlaid with Plastic Wood colored with pure lacquer. The colors are similar to those of a mallard duck. The manner in which this duck was carved (on the surface) made it unsuitable for inlay work.

Roughing out the duck (Fig. 220). The surplus wood around the head and the breast of the duck was removed with the saw shown in Fig. 221. Actually, Fig. 221 illustrates better than Fig. 220 how to rough out a carving with a saw. You have now only to round the sharp edges of the breast with the wood rasp to give it the round bulge that is characteristic of ducks. The photograph of the duck in Fig. 221 is the inlaid mallard duck in Fig. 216. Notice the exaggerated bulge of the breast in this photograph and also the slight uplift of the head and bill. Little points like this will make your wood carving resemble a duck. It is unnecessary to strive for

FIG. 214

FIG. 215

FIG. 216

Fig. 217

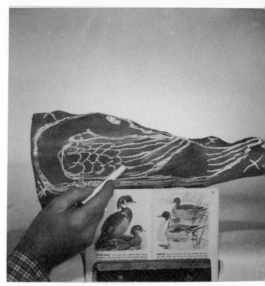

Fig. 218

Fig. 219

Fig. 220

an exact copy. The wood behind the duck's head (above the back) in Fig. 220 has been drilled out because it would have been difficult to reach there with the saw, due to the slight tilt of the duck's tail. This section of wood can now be knocked away with the wood gouge, and the carving, except for rasping, is roughed out.

The grooving of the wings of the finished carving in Fig. 220 not only does not add to it, but really detracts from it. Had the grooves been left off, it would be a fair carving. The wood has been stained with a maple stain, and the head is inlaid with color. The average duck carving does not require a base, but this one does or it would topple over. The base here seems to be about right for the carving. It is mounted to the base with a 1-inch wooden dowel pin, which, of course, is unnecessary. A ¼-inch dowel pin will prove to be sufficient.

Figure 222 demonstrates how to level the bottom of the duck carving with the hatchet. Notice the short grip on the hatchet. This makes it easier to control. After using the hatchet, rasp and sand the bottom until the carving will set level on a table or shelf. If you wish to sign your work, do it here on the bottom. Use a small or medium cutting burr in the small hand grinder and groove your name into the wood exactly the way you would print your name with a pencil. You might also inlay your name with a walnut- or mahogany-colored Plastic Wood.

Figure 223. Grooving in the wings with the rotary file. This same rotary file in the hand grinder was used to make the holes in the breast of the duck. Again, you have only to touch the wood with the file. Electricity does the rest.

The head and the breast of the duck at the bottom of Fig. 224 have been rasped and the wing and tail carved in and then sanded with the small sanding drum. Any other design for surface treatment that you can devise will almost surely be better than the above. There is no set rule for this. As long as the broad outline or shape of your carving resembles a duck, the minor details you add aren't important. Carve in any design you wish. In fact, if your duck were finished without surface treatment or details, it might make a better carving. This point is raised because details add little to a carving, and, as already mentioned, may detract from the carving. Should you decide to skip the surface details, then carve in only the eyes and bill of the duck, keeping the rest of the forms, wings, tail, etc., as simple as possible. As a final finish, you might try burnishing it with the large abrasive stone in the ¼-inch drill.

Compare the duck carvings in the illustration. Although no conscious attempt was made to make them look alike, notice the marked resemblance, especially in the head and body. The finished duck is about 2½ feet in length. The legs were constructed separately of wood, closely wrapped with piano wire, and then covered with liquid aluminum and liquid solder. Whenever possible avoid this sort of thing. It takes a lot of time and effort and money and yet adds nothing to the carving. These legs will somehow be forced out of the carving (they were set in with a contact cement), the holes will be plugged up with wooden dowel pins, and then sealed with a Plastic Wood that will blend with the rest of the carving (oak-colored Plastic Wood). The bottom of the carving will then be flattened out with a rasp and sanded so it can be set on a table or shelf without a base. Because of the size of this carving and its color (dark ivory), it is unusual, and it makes a different decoration for a summer home or den.

Figure 225. Rasping the duck. This large rasp is excellent for shaping the carving. It takes a bit longer than the hatchet or saw, but you will make fewer mistakes.

Figure 226. Sanding the carving with the Flexbac pad. The neck of the duck is much too big. All wood on the outside of the charcoal sketch will be ground away with the rotary file in the hand grinder. Notice how enough wood will be removed under the bill and in back of the head to permit later sanding with the small sanding drum in the ¼-inch drill.

Figure 227. Sanding the bill and eye with a small stone abrasive. The entire carving has been burnished with the large stone abrasive.

Notice how the holes in the breast of the duck at the bottom of Fig. 228 get smaller as they reach the head. These small holes were carved in with a smaller version of the rotary file that was used to make the larger ones. All these holes were then sanded or polished with the stone abrasive in the small hand grinder. Remember, you have only barely to touch these stone abrasives to the wood to sand it. The whole carving was then sanded lightly with the small sanding disc in the ¼-inch drill. You do this to clean up the carving of any discoloration and to remove charcoal marks, etc. Of course, the head of this duck (a young duck) is too large and the carving of the eye is unfortunate. The eye in the duck form above it is better. Notice that virtually all the carving on this weird duck form is against the grain. The wood inside the neck was drilled out. It would be an almost impossible job to do the grooving on this duck by hand, using a wood gouge and mallet. The sanding job alone, for remember it is all against the grain, would have taken days by hand. Yet, with the sanding drum and drill it takes only a bit of patience. Because this carving does not weigh much, it can be hung on a wall.

Don't let the prospect of carving the eyes and face of a bird or animal bother you. It is not as difficult as you may think. For a beginning the carving of the eye and bill in Fig. 229 will do. Surely there is nothing happening here that anyone, even without previous experience, cannot do. A very small rotary file is in the hand grinder. The eye and the bill later will be sanded with a small abrasive. After you have gained some experience, and, more important, self-confidence in handling the power tools, you can attempt a more realistic eye.

Notice the soft feathery look the burnishing gives the carving in Fig. 230. The eye and the bill on this side of the duck's head have been inlaid with walnut Plastic Wood. Later, this will be ground out again and the head will be finished as in Fig. 227. Again, notice the lift of the head and the bulging breast of the duck.

Pigeon

Figure 231 shows a pigeon preening itself. Except for the exaggerated length of the tail, the sketch is about life-size. For a simple carving like this, use a 10- or 12-inch section of a small log or branch of a tree. The wood from a dried-out fruit tree would be excellent. The sketch is 17 inches long, which is at least 5 or more inches too long.

Most of the roughing out was done with the hatchet, except the wood between the head and the body of the bird which is being sawed out (Fig. 232). In shaping the wood at the breast of the bird with the hatchet, work slowly and remove the surplus wood in small amounts. Don't expect to round the breast of the bird with one or two blows of the hatchet. Instead, remove the wood with the hatchet in layers, much as you would peel an orange, until the breast has a round, bulging look. With practice, this entire operation takes but a few minutes. Now go over the entire carving with the wood rasp. Originally it was intended to drill out the wood be-

FIG. 221

FIG. 222

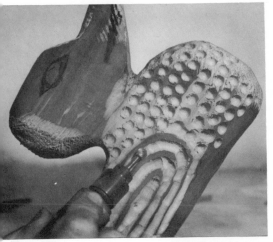

FIG. 223

FIG. 224

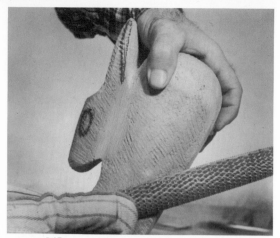

FIG. 225

FIG. 226

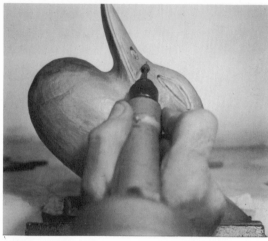

FIG. 227

FIG. 228

F<small>IG.</small> 229

F<small>IG.</small> 230

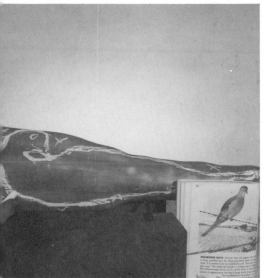

F<small>IG.</small> 231

F<small>IG.</small> 232

F<small>IG.</small> 233

F<small>IG.</small> 234

FIG. 235

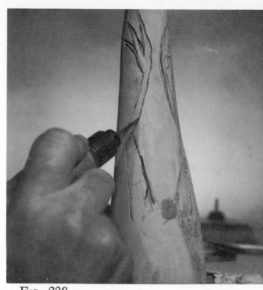

FIG. 236

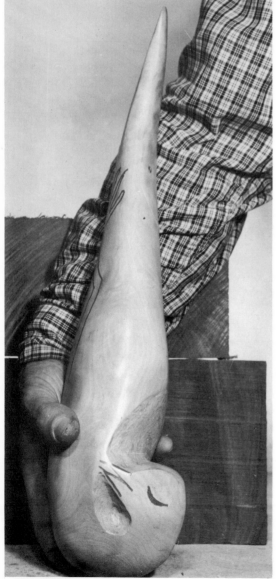

FIG. 238

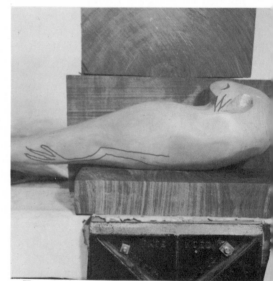

FIG. 237

FIG. 239

tween the head and the body with the ⅜-inch wood auger in the power drill, but at this point, the carving was changed to a sleeping or dead pigeon.

The carving in the circle of the neck where the rotary file is pointing in Fig. 233 is no more than ½ inch deep at the most. This is also true of the reverse side (Fig. 235). The head and the neck of the pigeon are not rounded as in life, but left more or less flat. And the edges or planes —the black charcoal lines in Figs. 233 to 235—will be left razor sharp. The reason for this is to bring out contrast with the rest of the body of the bird, which will be finished off perfectly round. This simple carving will be given a high finish— it will be sanded and then resanded, until even the tiniest scratch is removed. But to do a perfect sanding job where the rotary file is pointing in Figs. 233 and 235 would be difficult since this area of the carving is not easy to get at with the power tools or even by hand. Therefore, this area as well as that immediately behind the head on the back of the bird will be burnished with the large abrasive. Yet, the face and the back of the bird's head will be highly sanded like the body of the bird. These surfaces are flat and present no sanding problem. The result will be that the highly sanded and polished head of the bird will be framed, as it were, by roughly burnished wood. This burnishing, along with the sharp edges or planes of the head, will heighten the contrast with the smooth body of the pigeon.

Figure 236 shows the lifeless legs of the bird being carved in with a small cutting burr in the hand grinder. These legs, as well as the eye and bill of the bird, will be filled with light mahogany Plastic Wood.

Many wood carvers and woodworkers object to tampering with the natural wood. If you are one of these, skip the inlay work. The truth is that it adds little or nothing to a good carving. Yet, it can help somewhat to salvage a poor one. A ¼-inch hole was drilled into this carving between the legs for mounting purposes. But this carving, because it is a dead pigeon and because of the manner in which it is to be finished—well polished—requires no base. So the hole was plugged with a ¼-inch wooden dowel pin and then sealed up with oak Plastic Wood. Once the surplus Plastic Wood is sanded off, this hole will be barely visible.

This carving (Figs. 237 and 238) should be left on a table or mantel where people can pick it up and touch it if they choose. It is very light in weight, and, because of the very smooth finish, people will like to handle it. For the finishing, the carving was given at least six or seven coats of paste wax, and polished with the bonnet in the power drill between each coat.

In Fig. 239, a very small hole has been drilled through the neck of the bird and a wire strung through it so that the carving can be hung on a wall the same as a hunter hangs up his game. Perhaps this is stretching things a bit. If you were to decide not to hang the carving, use a kitchen match to plug up the hole, then seal the openings with oak or natural Plastic Wood.

Note: If the twist in the bird's head puzzles you or presents a problem, don't try it until you have first carved one where the bird's head is stretched out flat on the bird's back. In that case, the head would fill the wood marked X in front of the bird's head in Fig. 231.

8

Carving Animals

Dog

Most of the carvings in this chapter, finished and unfinished, as well as the sketches of animals, have the following in common: (1) The original shape of the wood suggested the carving. (2) The carvings are so fitted into the wood that little roughing out was necesary. (3) Either the head or the body of the animal is turned to give the carving action. In some instances, the teeth are exaggerated for the same reason. (4) They are either life-size or larger. (5) All are carved from cypress knees or roots. (6) They are animal forms and not meant to resemble any particular animal.

The legs, tail, and neck in the sketch in Fig. 240 follow the grain of the wood, so you can carve them in without fear of having them snap off.

The sketch in the center of Fig. 241 is a baby penguin. It is included here because it is sketched on the same piece of wood as the rabbit in Fig. 242. Not only would the penguin make a more interesting carving than the rabbit, but it would be a far easier one to make.

The rabbit sketched in Fig. 242 would not be a particularly difficult carving to make, because the drawing fills the wood fairly well. But remember that the amount of work you put into a carving is no guarantee that it will be a good one.

The head and chest of the rabbit (Fig. 243) were roughed out with the saw and hatchet. Knock out the remaining wood under the ears with the wood gouge, and the carving is ready for rasping.

No matter how weird the shape of the wood is, you can always figure out some animal form to fit into it. If you have a piece of wood, such as the cypress knees in Figs. 244 and 245, that suggests two different carvings, the fact that you select the one that involves the most work is no reason whatever why it should turn out to be a better carving than had you done the one that involved the lesser work.

In the right-hand figure in Fig. 246, all the wood between the legs and under the belly was removed with the ½-inch wood auger in the power gun. As you can see, the wood auger also was used to remove the wood behind the animal's neck. The rasping of the tail and hind legs is partly completed. This wood is soft and easy to rasp. Continue to sketch even after you have begun to carve. It is a good way to decide what you intend to do next. The sketching behind the neck of the dog means that this area is to be rasped off. The finished carving on the left has been bleached. The teeth are inlaid with aluminum and the collar is inlaid with various colors of melted lacquer. The face is inlaid with Plastic Wood.

Here again, in Fig. 247, is an almost perfect example of what is meant by making a carving the natural way. Remove the wood marked X between the ears of the

Fig. 240

Fig. 241

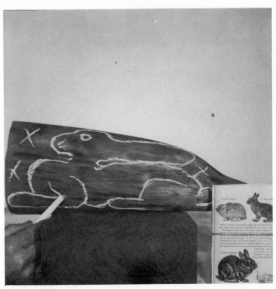

Fig. 242

F<small>IG</small>. 243

F<small>IG</small>. 244

F<small>IG</small>. 245

F<small>IG</small>. 246

dog, and, with the wood gouge and mallet, dig out about an inch between the front legs where the chalk is pointing, and the carving practically is finished. To complete it, you have only barely to indicate such forms as the hips, the tail, the front legs, and the face of the animal. At no point would you have to carve deeper than an inch to realize the finished carving.

If you are wondering just how to begin carving the face of an animal, Fig. 248 shows you. You start by doing what you see here. Of course, this isn't exactly the way an animal's face looks, but it is close enough so the carving vaguely can be identified as an animal form. The wood between the ears of this carving can be removed either with the saw or the wood auger in the power gun.

Notice how the finished carving in Fig. 249 is leaning forward and how this, plus the twist of the head, puts life into it. The carving leans forward because of the way the base of this piece of wood was sawed before carving was begun. For example, if you were to remove the wood below the sketched line in the uncarved piece where the chalk is pointing, then this piece of wood would lean forward also, and, as a result, anything you carved in it would be leaning forward.

The carvings so far have been fairly large. If you'd like to try something smaller, the branch of a tree could be used for the sketch in Fig. 250. The sketch fills the wood; thus there is very little roughing out to do. The gopher in the center of Fig. 251 is an easy carving with which to start. It, too, can be carved from a branch or section of a small log.

The only difference between the carving in Fig. 252 and the one in Fig. 246 is that, with the exception of the head, ·it has been rasped all over. It is good to do this, because it gives you a better idea of the over-all appearance of the figure. The

legs and the neck are too large, and the carving is far from finished, but it is less confusing than before rasping. At least now you can tell what has to be done to it.

The animal form at the rear of this illustration, and those in the background of Figs. 256 and 260 were carved from cypress driftwood from the shores of Lake Pontchartrain, near New Orleans, Louisiana. All the carvings are about 4 feet in length, and, in each case, the carving carefully follows the silhouette or outline of the wood. These are unusual pieces of wood. The main problem was to decide what could be carved out of them. By sketching on the wood with a piece of chalk, these forms eventually were evolved.

You easily can figure out how the actual carving was done on the background figure in Fig. 252. The face (African Negro in influence) was inlaid with aluminum. The head and neck were stained walnut, the body, maple, and the inside of the grooving outlining the tail, back, and neck, red. The edges of these grooves were then stained black. All but the grooving outlining the animal was then waxed. The red stain in the grooves was made by adding dry red color to the maple stain. The base, which appears appropriate, is ordinary pine painted a flat black. "Rather unusual" is the general comment from those who have seen it.

There is no set way to mount a carving as you can see in Figs. 253–255. Drilling into the carving at different angles enables you to experiment until you find the position best suited to the carving. Notice the black guide line on the left front foot of the rabbit. A hole for mounting purposes was drilled here also.

The entire carving of the dog in Fig. 256 has been sanded with a medium sanding disc and the head sketched in. The rasp marks on the neck cannot be reached with the large sanding disc be-

FIG. 247

FIG. 248

FIG. 249

FIG. 250

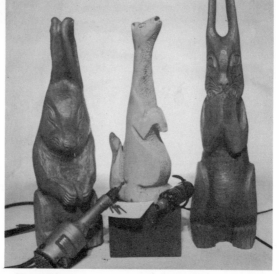

FIG. 251

FIG. 252

FIG. 253

FIG. 254

FIG. 255

111

cause of the tail of the dog; but any of the sanding drums in the foreground could have been used.

The only roughing out that was necessary on the carving in the background was to round the nose of the animal with a wood rasp and to drill out the wood in the mouth which was then inlaid with Plastic Wood. The body has been grooved. Except for the head, the rest of this carving is hollow. In some places, the wooden shell of the body is no more than ¼ inch thick. As a result, the carving weighs very little.

An arrangement such as Fig. 257 over the fireplace of a den looks well.

Because of the size, 27 inches, and the shape, the carving in Fig. 258 would be difficult to mount on a base. When you are confronted with a similar problem, try mounting it on the wall.

Seldom will the addition of gadgets, as in Fig. 259, add to a carving, and, therefore, the practice should be avoided. The pine base probably weighs more than the carving.

The eyes, nose, and mouth of the dog in the foreground of Fig. 260 have been grooved in and the front legs have been rasped so they would not look so awkward as they do in Fig. 256. The entire carving, face and all, was then burnished with a stone abrasive in the power gun. The twist in the tail of the animal is very slight, yet notice how much it does for the carving.

The unfinished carving in the background is a dog that has been run over by a truck. The tire marks have been sketched on the animal's back with crayon. While it would be carrying realism a bit far, these tire marks could be burned in with an electric soldering iron or burner instead of being carved in. Or, since burning wood with an electric soldering iron is a very slow process, the marks could first be sketched in lightly with a medium cutting burr in the hand grinder and then retraced with the burning iron.

Figure 261 is a polar bear cub. The wood at which the finger is pointing will be knocked off with a wood gouge, shaped to fit the hole where the thumb is pointing, and then hammered in. The edges then will be sealed with light mahogany Plastic Wood which matches the color of the wood. When finished, it will be difficult, if not impossible, to tell where the hole was originally. This cypress cross section is 3 inches thick and roughly about the size of a bear cub. Other than drilling out the wood between the legs of the animal, there is very little surplus wood to be eliminated in order to realize the shape.

Figures 262 and 263. Only the head and face of this piece of wood will be carved. No attempt will be made to round or shape the legs and body. Instead, the grain of the wood, not too apparent in these illustrations, will be emphasized. Consequently, the power gun and Flexbac pad will do most of the work.

The surface of the carving of the dog in Fig. 264, with the exception of the eyes, nose, and ears, was scratched with the medium burr in the grinder as demonstrated in Fig. 265. However, the burnished figure in Fig. 260 looks better, so these scratches will be sanded off and the carving reburnished. The entire surface of the howling dog in the background was grooved with the rotary file and then sanded with the small sanding drum. It was waxed with a dark paste wax, which accounts for its color. The grooving on the chest resembles a spider's web. Notice how it is almost perfectly centered on the breast of the animal. Obviously, to achieve this effect requires a great deal of preliminary sketching, because the grooving more or less follows the anatomy of the animal.

The scratched surface of any carving can be somewhat improved by a light sanding as shown in Fig. 266.

Notice in Fig. 267 how the grooving

Fig. 256

Fig. 257

Fig. 258

FIG. 259

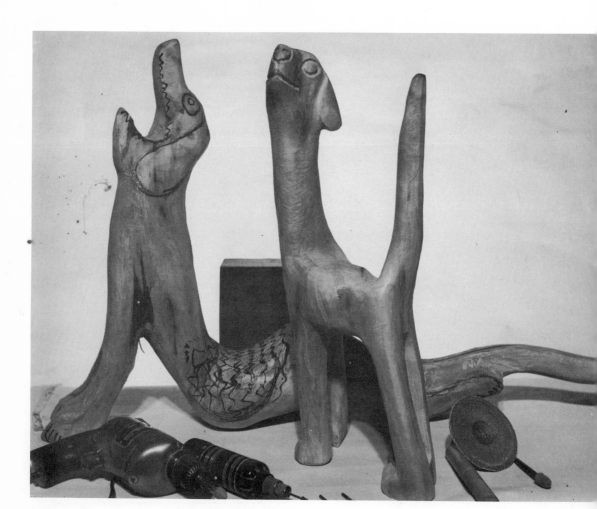

FIG. 260

114

Fɪɢ. 262

Fɪɢ. 263

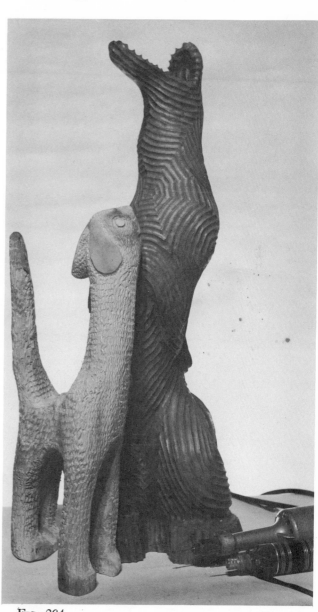

Fɪɢ. 264

115

FIG. 265

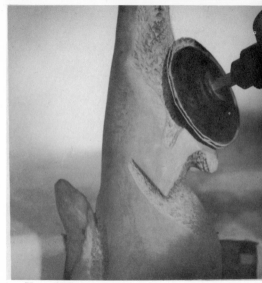

FIG. 266

FIG. 267

generally follows the anatomy of the animals. The howling dog is 30 inches, and the squirrel is 20 inches.

Lion

The emphasis in this chapter will be limited largely to the sketching. The face of the lion in the sketch in Fig. 268 will be similar to the one of the smaller lion on the right. There is a slight bulge in the wood where the nose is sketched in. Always take advantage of these irregularities in the formation of the wood. The right front leg is another such instance in this sketch.

Except for the tail, Fig. 269 indicates how the small lion looked when first sketched on the wood. Remove the wood marked *XXX* on the front legs of this sketch to the depth of about an inch, and the feet are formed. The hip can be indicated by grooving a line about an inch deep where the chalk is pointing, and then curving the lion's body gradually into this groove. There is not enough wood here to carve in the ears, so choose an animal in which the ears are not prominent—such as a monkey.

The mane of the small lion in Fig. 268 was carved with a medium rotary file (Fig. 270), and then sanded with a small abrasive stone.

Figure 271, center. Since you cannot reach behind the animal's right front leg with the saw in order to remove the wood marked *xxxx*, drill it out with the wood auger in the power gun. The left leg of this carving (not visible) is pressed against the body of the animal.

The carving of the seated cat on the left in Fig. 271 was sketched as shown in Fig. 272. However, instead of curving the tail up the animal's back, the wood visible behind the pocket book will be used for it.

The carving on the right in Fig. 271 looked as shown in Fig. 273 when it was first sketched on the wood. The finished work is 33 inches tall, but only 2 or 3 inches thick at the base, which means that it has to be mounted on a wider base or it would topple over. Since this base is thin, it was fastened to the carving with wood screws. The carving weighs but a few pounds and easily can be hung on a wall, in which case, naturally, the base should be removed. The sketches in Figs. 272 and 273 were not done on the same pieces of wood as those from which the finished carvings were made. Instead, similarly shaped pieces of wood were used.

In the center figure of Fig. 274, the carving of the face and the mane has been started with the large grinder. The cat carving to the right was stained a reddish brown. You do this by mixing some dry red color with walnut stain. The face was inlaid with aluminum and Plastic Wood, and after sanding the carving was waxed.

The surface of the squirrel on the left in Fig. 274 was first scratched with a cutting burr in the grinder and then sanded lightly with the small sanding disc (Fig. 275). The eyes, teeth, and the inside of the ears were stained a darker color than the rest of the carving, before the entire piece was waxed.

The outlines of the eyes in the center carving of Fig. 276 were made by tracing two oval shapes on the face. Additional carving of the eyes will be illustrated in Fig. 279. Notice the position of the front legs in the two finished carvings. In the one on the left, they are inside the hips; in the other carving—a monkey—they are on the outside. This monkey carving could have been fitted into the piece of wood out of which the lion is being carved.

Once you've completed a carving and decide you don't like it, instead of throwing it away or destroying it, try carving something else out of it. The carving in Fig. 278 was carved out of the figure in Fig. 277.

The eyelids of the lion in Fig. 279 were first grooved in with the small cutting burr,

FIG. 268

FIG. 269

FIG. 270

Fɪɢ. 271

Fɪɢ. 272

Fɪɢ. 273

Fig. 274

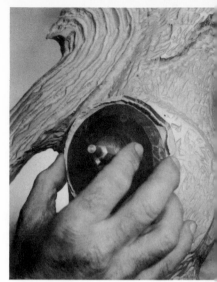

Fig. 275

Fig. 277

Fig. 276

Fig. 278

120

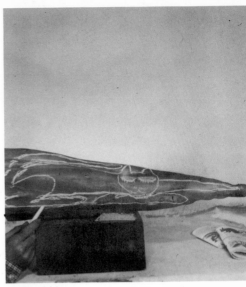

FIG. 280

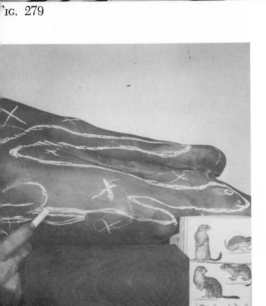

FIG. 282

FIG. 283

and the inside of the eye was then shaped with the small sanding abrasive. The body of the lion has been burnished.

Figures 280 and 281. Most of the carvings in this book were carved with the cypress knee sitting on its base. Almost as many different forms can be carved into the wood by laying it on its side. The sleeping cat in Fig. 280 would make a good carving, and eventually will be carved exactly as sketched.

Never scratch the body and face of a carving as is demonstrated in the piece on the left of Fig. 282. It was done with a small cutting burr in the hand grinder. Fortunately, it can be sanded off without too much trouble. Except for the tail and the right front leg, the rest of this carving can be recarved into almost anything—cat, dog, or monkey. For example, remove the mane of the lion with a wood gouge or the hatchet and carve in the neck of an animal. The carving in the face of the lion is no deeper than $\frac{1}{2}$ of an inch, so this can be rasped off in a few minutes, then sanded, and a fresh start made. In fact, the only things that cannot be altered in this

carving, as already stated, are the right front leg and the tail, because they have been more or less separated from the rest of the carving.

Figure 283 shows the face detail of the lioness on the right in Fig. 282. This lioness carving is just 1 inch or so short of 4 feet. Yet, since it weighs no more than around 10 pounds, it can be hung on a wall with a small eye hook twisted into the back of the head. All carving on the tail (see Fig. 282), which extends at least a foot above the head of the lioness, is against the grain of the wood. This lioness, surely one of the best carvings in the book, is no more difficult to make than the other lion carving on the left in Fig. 282. And in spite of its size, it involved no more work. The cypress knee from which the carving was made, like many others in the book, resembled a triangle or pyramid, if looked at from the base. The tail in this carving fills the top part of this triangle, and the body, the base part. This carving—tan or slightly reddish in color—makes a handsome wall decoration. The face is a very easy one to carve.

Carving Masks

Animal masks are easy to carve because you can do anything you wish, just so your carving vaguely resembles an animal or bird. In fact, the more unusual you make your carving the better. Look at pictures of masks from Africa, the South Seas, or the Pacific Northwest, and you will get an idea of how truly fantastic some of them are. Notice in particular *how* they were carved and not necessarily what they represent. Instead, use American birds and animals for subject matter. Exaggerate the particular features of the animal head you have in mind as much as possible. You might begin by making a caricature of the animal; then go on from there and add any details you develop.

Note: Once you've looked at some of these primitive masks, it is difficult not to be influenced by them to some extent. Especially is this true of African Negro masks.

Goat

The sketch in Fig. 284 is just short of 2 feet high. Most of the wood is being used, and what little has to be removed can either be sawed off or chopped off with the hatchet. Remember to try to make your carving conform to the shape of the piece of wood you are using. The animal mask carving on the left was carved from a 2-foot section of cypress. The design, which was carved in almost entirely with the large cutting burr in the

Dumore hand grinder (*see* Fig. 287), was modeled after designs used by the natives of the South Seas in their animal carvings. The eyes are unfortunate to say the least. Otherwise, because of the rough manner in which it is carved, and, more, because of its size, it does have a certain vigor. A carving like this belongs on the wall of a hunting camp.

Remove the wood marked X in Fig. 285 with a hatchet and you are ready to start carving. You could carve either ears or horns out of the two prongs.

The carving will be completed, but notice in Fig. 286 how it will be changed in the carving process. Never hesitate to make changes even after carving has begun.

The lower part of the mask or jaw of the right-hand carving in Fig. 288 was shaped with the saw. The wood on the outside was then removed with the wood gouge and mallet so that the face of the animal projects out from the grooving in the background about an inch. All carving was done with the rotary file in the grinder. The saw was used to shape the horns and ears.

The somewhat vicious look on the face of the finished mask to the left in this illustration is due largely to the way in which the eyes are inlaid and the manner in which the nose is carved. The base for this carving should be slightly larger.

The carving of the eyes and of the out-

FIG. 284

FIG. 285

FIG. 286

Fig. 287

288

Fig. 289

line of the nose of the mask in Fig. 288 was done exactly as you see it being done in Fig. 289. The grooving is about ¼ inch deep. You merely trace over the lines of your sketch with the rotary file, and the electricity does the rest.

Notice how the sketch in Fig. 290 has been changed from the one in Fig. 286. The grooving with the small cutting burr is at least ¼ inch deep. The teeth will be carved in with this same cutting burr.

To hang a mask carving on the wall, twist an eye hook into it so that it will hang at the angle you want (*see* Fig. 291).

The face of the mask in Fig. 292 projects out from the wall about 8 inches. It is held to the wall with a wire. Since cypress wood is very light in weight, hanging these carvings presents no problem.

In the illustration on the right of Fig. 293, the ears and horns were carved with the hand grinder and then sanded with the small sanding drum in the power gun. The wood around the eyes and nose was pushed back or carved away about ¼ of an inch so that the eyes and nose project out from the face of the carving. Use the rotary file in the hand grinder to do this, and then sand with a medium sanding disc. Use the cut-down rubber backing pad because it enables you to sand where you cannot reach with the larger sanding discs. In places where you cannot reach with this small disc, use the sanding drum.

Figure 294 shows about how the finished carving on the left in Fig. 293 looked when it was first sketched. Obviously, changes were made once carving was begun.

You either can drill out the wood between the horns of a carving with a wood auger in the power gun or remove it with a saw. The saw in Fig. 295 saws with or against the grain with equal ease. Whenever possible, use the saw because it is quicker and easier than using the wood

auger. If the V-shaped wedge you are trying to remove from your carving does not come to a point, drill out the bottom with the wood auger as was done in this illustration. The saw depicted was not large enough to saw to this depth, because of the frame holding the blade. A much larger version of this same saw was used. Notice how the carving has been changed from the sketch in Fig. 294. This carving, when finished, will resemble the head of a rabbit. Although at least ½ of an inch separates the tips of the rabbit's ears, they will appear to draw together because the grain of the wood comes to a gradual point.

In Fig. 296, the rabbit's head is being shaped with the hatchet. The cutting edge of the tool is tempered and so razor sharp that only a slight pressure is required to remove the wood. Notice the short grip on the handle. This enables you to have complete control of what you are doing at all times.

In Fig. 297, the thin chalk marks on the edges of the grooves are a reminder not to carve them away. The carving here is similar to carving scales on a fish. The slope of the wood in the groove curves in and slightly under the groove on top. The wood where the teeth will be has been carved away to a depth of ¼ inch with the rotary file, so that the teeth, when the carving is completed, will appear to be set in the carving. By all means, emphasize the teeth in these animal masks. They not only put some life into the mask, but create a weird effect.

The carving above the eyes is the reverse of the carving below, so turn your carving around in the vise as demonstrated in Fig. 298. This makes it easier to shape the grooves.

The face of the center carving in Fig. 299 was sanded lightly with the small sanding disc (shown in the lower right-hand corner) in order to make sketching

FIG. 290

FIG. 291

FIG. 292

FIG. 293

Fig. 294

Fig. 295

Fig. 296

Fig. 297

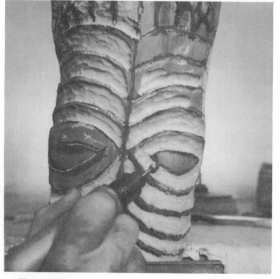

Fig. 298

easier. Notice how the teeth are carved so they appear to stick out of the carving. They were carved with the medium cutting burr in the small grinder, and then sanded with a stone abrasive. Because you are using power tools, you can sink these teeth as deep as an inch into the carving, and not have it involve any more work.

The goat carving on the right was carved from a cypress fence post. By drilling a hole down through the center of this carving, or for that matter through any of the three in this illustration, you could make a lamp out of it.

If the wood you are using is reasonably soft, shape the eyeball with a stone abrasive in the hand grinder as indicated in Fig. 300. Naturally, it takes longer to shape it with this abrasive, but you are less likely to make a mistake as you might if you were using a cutting burr or rotary file. What gives the face of this carving its peculiar texture or appearance is the fact that it was burnished against the grain of the wood. Notice the contrast between the rough carved ears and horns and the waxed and polished face.

The teeth in Fig. 301 are being carved with a small rotary file because they will be inlaid with lacquer. Since the melted lacquer is difficult to control, the grooves must be made wider. One side of the carving has been sanded with the small sanding disc in the illustration. This is done mainly to remove pencil or crayon marks and to clean up the carving. No pressure has to be put on the power tool in order to perform this operation. You have only barely to touch the carving.

Do whatever sketching you have in mind with a soft lead pencil—*see* left side of center mask in Fig. 302—and then trace over it with a small or medium cutting burr in the hand grinder. These grooves do not have to be more than $\frac{1}{16}$ of an inch deep. Don't worry about how fuzzy the grooving appears at this stage; it will be eliminated as you trace over the grooves again with a small stone abrasive in the hand grinder.

The goat carving on the left is mounted on a stained 1-inch wooden dowel pin. It is difficult to imagine how else this carving might have been mounted, because of the manner in which it was carved. This head was bleached white, and, when thoroughly dry, was sanded here and there to allow the original wood to show through. However, enough bleach was left in an attempt to give the carving the appearance of a marble fragment dug up out of the earth.

In Fig. 303, the black lacquer stick was melted with the torch directly over the grooves in the teeth and allowed to drip and run into them. The white lacquer stick was then hold to the flame, and, as the end of the stick began to melt, was dabbed on the teeth. The addition of lacquer to only a portion of the carving does not seem right, so unless you're prepared to lacquer the entire carving, it would perhaps be best to leave it off entirely. However, since color definitely adds something to an animal mask, other suggestions will be made in the paragraphs which follow.

The three carvings in Fig. 304, whatever their merits as carvings, had they been made with hand tools would represent an enormous amount of work. With power tools, however, no more work was involved than holding the grinder in the hand and guiding the tool over the surface of the wood. It is not much more work than sketching in the design with a pencil in the first place.

The carvings on each side of the animal mask were given a coat of Firzite cut with benzine and waxed. This accounts for the darker color of the wood. The mask could be improved by staining or bleaching the teeth and horns white, the eyes a dark red

FIG. 299

FIG. 300

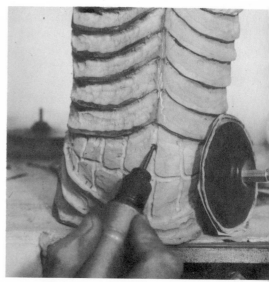

FIG. 301

FIG. 302

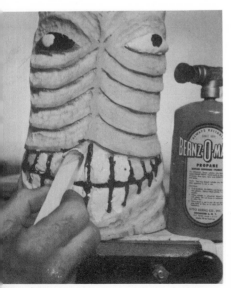

FIG. 303

FIG. 304

(maple), and the rest of the carving a dark walnut.

There are several products on the market that can be used for bleaching or decolorizing wood. However, the application of some of these bleaches is a rather involved and messy process, and, with at least one product, rubber gloves must be used to avoid injury to the hands. So perhaps it is best to use stains only.

The body of the young goat on the left in Fig. 305 was bleached or decolorized, and, when thoroughly dry, was sanded lightly and waxed. A dark walnut stain was used on the head, and the eyes were inlaid with white Plastic Wood.

Fox

This is one of the easiest carvings to make in the entire book. If you select the right piece of wood you can't possibly miss on this one. Use that section of a small tree or a large branch (or driftwood) where it comes to a fork as in Fig. 306. Such tree formations are very common and not hard to find, but you must get out in a woods or along a lake to do so. Naturally, you are not going to find such a piece of wood in a lumberyard. What makes this carving so easy to make is that the wood you select largely will determine the shape of the carving. The head of a fox was used here as a guide. Originally, it was intended to carve in the ears—there is adequate wood—but these were altered to horns as you will see presently. Remember, in carving an animal mask, there are no set rules to go by. The fact that a fox does not have horns is not a bit important.

All wood marked X in Fig. 306 was removed with the hatchet and wood rasp (Fig. 307). The grooving of the eyes and the nose is about $\frac{1}{4}$ inch deep, that on the outline of the jaw at least $\frac{1}{2}$ inch. The wood marked X below the nose of the animal can be removed with a saw or wood gouge. This will cause the jaw of the carving to project out from the neck at least an inch or so.

The horns of the fox in the center of Fig. 308 were carved in with a rotary file as shown in Fig. 309. Again notice the thin ridges of wood between the grooves. These ridges will be brought to a sharp edge when the grooves are sanded with the small sanding drum. The neck of the mask will be grooved in the same manner as the horns. Since the grain of the wood runs from the bottom up, all this grooving is against or across the grain.

The entire carving (Fig. 310) has been sanded with the small sanding disc, and then the face of the mask was burnished as indicated in Fig. 311. The eyes and nostrils were carved in with the small cutting burr in the grinder and then sanded with the stone abrasive.

Most masks are improved by staining. This one would look better if stained a flat, dull black and hung on a light-colored wall. It is 27 inches high. Notice how, once this carving was roughed out (Fig. 307), most of the rest of the work was done with power tools. This means that the size of your carving isn't too important in relation to the amount of work involved—electricity furnishes most of the energy. It does mean that a large carving may take a little more time and patience, but because you are using power tools, it is nowhere near what would be required if you were making a carving solely with hand tools.

The difference in physical labor between making a small or a large carving isn't important enough to give it a thought. There is, however, a personal preference. If you prefer to make your carvings smaller, then by all means do so—the actual size of a carving proves nothing. Furthermore, methods of procedure are the same no matter what the size of your carving. The author, however, finds it easier to work with larger forms.

Fɪɢ. 305

Fɪɢ. 306

Fɪɢ. 307

Fɪɢ. 308

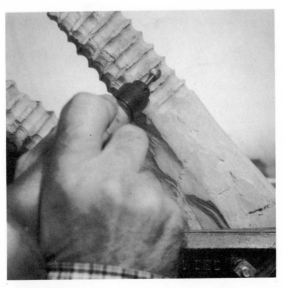

Fɪɢ. 309

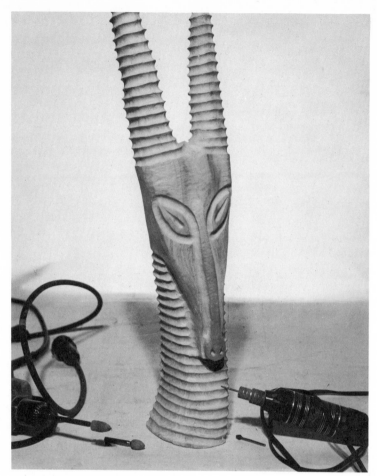

FIG. 310

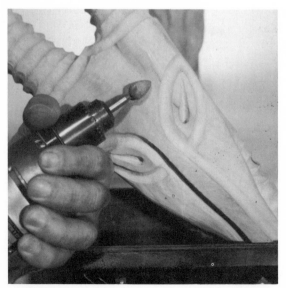

FIG. 311

Human Head

The human head will be difficult to carve only if you insist on trying to carve an exact likeness. To convince you how unimportant this realism is, the next time you are window-shopping study carefully the mannequins in the windows. Some of these are amazingly realistic, but this isn't the sort of thing that you want to carve. So forget about realism and concentrate only on making the wood you are using *look like a human head.*

Young Girl

A 12-inch section of a small round log can be used for carving the girl sketched in Fig. 312. Most of the wood marked X can be removed with the saw. The hair and the eyebrows in the finished carving are inlaid with Plastic Wood. This head is a good example of what to avoid.

Although there isn't enough wood in Figs. 313 and 314 really to carve a head in the round, there is still enough to suggest a head. For this very reason, the head sketched in these illustrations is both more interesting and will be easier to carve than the head in Fig. 312. Notice particularly the chalk marks suggesting the hair in Fig. 314.

The saw was used to shape the top of the head of the center carving in Fig. 315. All that is needed now to complete rounding the head is a little rasping. If you learn how to use the saw, it is not necessary to spend a lot of time chipping away with the wood gouge. Since this piece of wood is soft, the neck was roughed out entirely with the wood rasp. The grooving outlining the eyes, nose, and mouth is about ¼ inch deep.

Notice in Fig. 316 how just by tracing over the chalk marks with the rotary file, the head begins to take shape. The grooved lines representing the hair will be curved up in the back of the head to represent an upsweep.

The grooving in the two finished carvings in Fig. 315 was made with a small rotary file and then sanded with a small stone abrasive as demonstrated in Fig. 317. The influence here, of course, is African Negro. Carving a design like this is not as difficult as it may appear. In fact, it is far easier than trying to carve a realistic face. You first carve or, more accurately, rough in the features. You have only barely to indicate these features—nose, eyes, mouth, etc.—and, since you are making a mask, the more crudely you do this the better, Then, with the small abrasive drum, sand the carving until it is smooth enough to permit sketching. For a beginning, you might try this: With a piece of chalk, mark the center of the forehead, eyes, nose, mouth, chin, and cheeks. Now draw a small circle around each mark and continue until the entire surface of the face is covered. The two groups of circles comprising the eyes gradually will join at the ridge of the nose. You will then have to join or blend these two circles with those comprising the nose itself, and so on until all the circles have been joined together. Do not strive for perfection. No one is going to pick up your carving and scrutinize it to see if you made any mistakes.

No matter what rotary file you use, it eventually will get as dull as any tool. Instead of discarding it, utilize it in making a carving such as the one in the center of Fig. 318. By using a dull accessory to carve and shape the features of the face, you won't make as many mistakes because the dull accessory obviously is not as efficient as a sharp one. It takes longer, but it is safer. The carving in this face at no point exceeds more than ½ inch, and in most places is only ¼ inch. In other words, the features are only suggested. The mouth and the eyes, for example, do not project out more than ¼ inch from the face. The dark spots on the cheeks,

Fig. 312

Fig. 313

Fig. 314

Fig. 315

FIG. 316

FIG. 317

FIG. 318

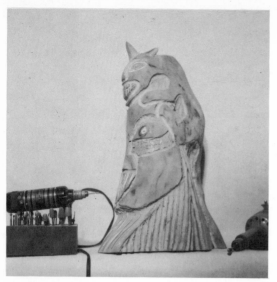

FIG. 319

FIG. 320

FIG. 321

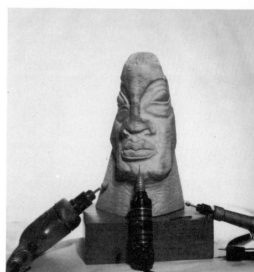

FIG. 322

FIG. 323

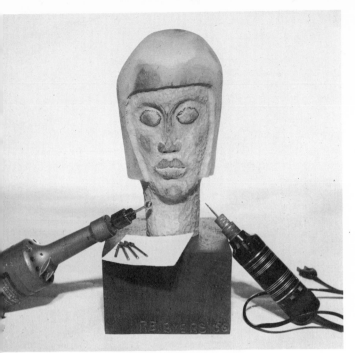

FIG. 324

FIG. 325

FIG. 326

FIG. 327

eyes, and mouth are the outside of the wood. This will give you an idea of how little actual carving has been done.

The unfinished carving on the left is hollow. The hair on the one to the right is inlaid with black lacquer, and the face has been burnished. The comb is curved and is not much more than ⅛ inch thick.

Figures 319 to 323 show how a carving can be changed even after work has begun. Nor is there anything final about the carving in Fig. 323. It would only take a few minutes with a rasp to erase the face. You then would still have a solid chunk of wood with which to begin another piece of work.

In Fig. 324, the neck of the girl has been shortened and the hair sanded. The nostrils were carved with the small cutting burr in the small grinder. To carve

in the eyes as sketched would be somewhat difficult because they allow no room for error. Instead, carve them in as shown in Fig. 325. Use the small cutting burr to carve, or more accurately, to scratch in the lips as shown in the illustration. No attempt will be made to erase the tool marks on the face.

To finish this carving (Fig. 326), the hair should be given a thorough sanding and then waxed in order to bring out the contrast with the more or less rough carving on the face. After carving in the outline of the eye with the small cutting burr, shape the eyeball itself with a stone abrasive as shown in Fig. 327. The base in Fig. 326 is much too large. One-half this size would be about right. The carving is 10 inches high.

Lacquering

Lacquering on wood is not difficult. All you do is melt the sticks of lacquer with a torch and let them drip or spread on the carving. But, since the lacquer dries almost instantly, it is difficult to control or manage and you must learn to work fast. There is no time for detail work.

Fish Discs

All eight carvings in Figs. 328 and 329 were finished differently on each side. Their brilliant colors—red, black, white, blue, and green—do not show up in the black-and-white illustrations. A group of carvings such as this can be mounted so that they can be viewed from either side; thus, you really have sixteen carvings, and not just eight.

In order to place one color next to the other, first groove the carving as shown in Fig. 330. Do not sand after grooving, because the rougher the carving, the better the lacquer will grip the wood.

The colors in Fig. 331 are red, black, white, and blue. The grooving gives you at least some control over the colors, but not much. As the lacquer melts, you spread it over the grooves.

Should the brittle lacquer stick break, use a pair of pliers to hold the broken pieces to the torch (Fig. 332).

If you are going to drip the color on the carving, then first rough it up as in Fig. 333.

Hold the lacquer to the torch over the carving and let the melted lacquer drip on it as demonstrated in Fig. 334. Use as many different colors as you wish. Once the carving is covered, put the flame of the torch directly on the colors, and they will blend. In this illustration, the colors were overheated, causing them to boil and bubble. The best way is just to brush the colors lightly with the flame. Once they begin to melt and flow into each other, remove the flame. If the colors do not blend the way you wish, let them cool for a moment and try again. You will gain nothing by overheating the lacquer.

In lacquering over grooves, you can hold the torch directly to the lacquer, and, as it melts, trace it over the grooves as in Fig. 335.

The carvings in Fig. 336 are those previously inlaid with Plastic Wood. Instead of discarding them, scratch the surface and use them to experiment with melted lacquer.

The top carving in Fig. 337 was covered entirely with white lacquer. This was easy, since you are working with only one color. Black lacquer was then melted and allowed to drip on the white. The lacquer in the lower carving was applied as shown in Fig. 338. Holding the torch this close to the carving may cause the lacquer to sputter and ignite. When it does, simply blow it out. The colors used in Fig. 339 are blue, black, white, green, and red. Melt the lacquer and apply it to the carv-

FIG. 328

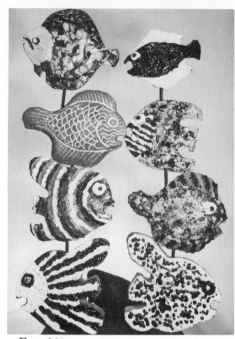

FIG. 329

FIG. 330

FIG. 331

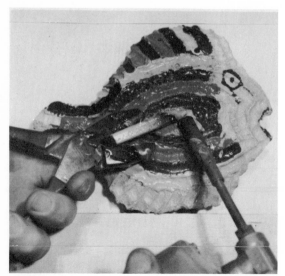

FIG. 332

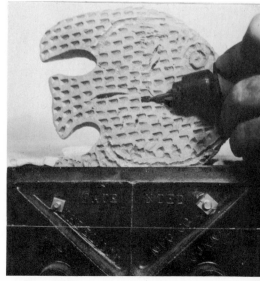

FIG. 333

142

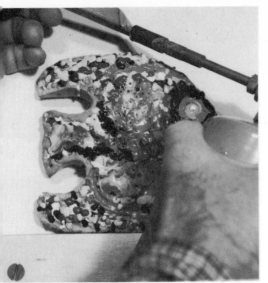

FIG. 334

FIG. 335

FIG. 336

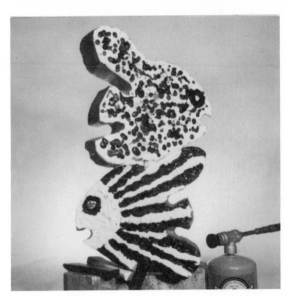

FIG. 337

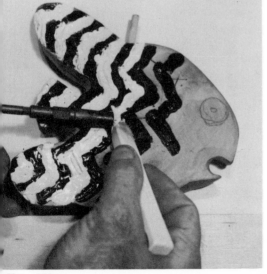

FIG. 338

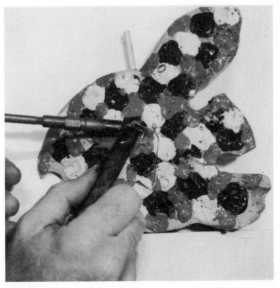

FIG. 339

ing in different places. Then, using another color, do the same thing. Continue with each color until the entire carving is covered. If you wish, you can then apply the torch directly to the colors and blend them together.

Fish in the Round

The tiny holes in the carving (Fig. 340) were made by striking the carving with hard blows, using the rounded side of the large wood rasp. The melted lacquer fills these holes, causing it to grip the surface of the wood more firmly (Fig. 341). Even if you didn't do this, the melted lacquer would still adhere to the wood; but this is one way of insuring that it will stay there permanently. The lacquer is brittle, so if you dropped the carving on a hard surface, it probably would crack the inlay work. You could remove the lacquer from the carving with a wood rasp, but it would involve work and you would dull the rasp to some extent. One way of getting most of it off the carving is to remelt it with the torch and let it run off. Lacquer is a reasonably permanent material to work in, and a carving done in it will probably be around as long as the person who creates the piece.

The mouth, eyes, gills, and fins will be inlaid with black lacquer, the rest of the fish with white. Had the entire carving, except for the eyes, been done in white, it would have been much better. You could then add the black dots to make the carving resemble a speckled trout. These black dots are very easy to apply. You merely heat the end of the lacquer stick and then touch it to the carving. Since inlaying a carving in all one color is easy—in this case only the white lacquer is used before the black dots are added—you only would have the eyes to worry about. You do this by letting the melted lacquer drip and run into the grooves of the eye. The one important point to remember is to

keep the over-all design of the carving you intend to inlay as simple as possible, and, at least in the beginning, do not use too many different colors.

If your carving is all inlaid in melted white lacquer, you can always touch it up with the tube of Plastic Porcelain you see in Fig. 342. However, this Plastic Porcelain is slightly whiter than the melted white lacquer, so you will have to apply the torch directly to the carving and force the porcelain to blend with the lacquer. If you didn't do this, your carving would look patched up and amateurish.

A very good project to start with would be the rabbit in Fig. 343. First finish carving in the holes in the face to match those on the body, groove in the eyes, and then cover the entire carving with melted white lacquer. The holes on the surface naturally would show through the white lacquer, and this would add to the interest of the piece. You then could fill in the eyes and possibly the inside of the ears with a light-pink lacquer, and, as a final touch, dab a spot of pink lacquer on the nose. This would be a very easy inlay to make; except for a little pink in the eyes, ears, and nose, you are using only one color, white. A carving roughly shaped like a dove or pigeon could also be inlaid all in white, with the eye in pink.

Notice the sketched rabbit in the illustration. That a rabbit does not sit in this position is not important. Do not ever worry about such a minor detail. Note how it fills the wood, and how easy it would be to rough out this carving. You could do most of it with the saw and rasp. Other carvings which can be fitted into this same piece of wood are shown in Chapter 8, "Carving Animals."

Young Girl

Fig. 344 is a mannequin, size 22½, used by the millinery trade. It is made of laminated balsa wood and weighs no more than a football. The advantage in using this mannequin is that it is already roughed out, and carving can begin immediately. These mannequins also come in at least five or more sizes. The one being sketched in Fig. 344 is about average in size. They can be purchased at any millinery supply house, or perhaps a department store or a women's hat shop in your neighborhood will have a damaged one around which they will sell you. Since you are going to carve it and then inlay it with lacquer, it doesn't matter how much it is damaged. The groove in the mannequin in Fig. 345 was put there by the manufacturer. The wood at which the finger is pointing will be removed, as will some of the wood in the back of the neck. Of course, you could do this in just the opposite way: let the wood below the groove alone and shrink the head above it. If you were to carve the head smaller, and not touch the wood below the grooved line, you very easily could make this mannequin look like the head of a small Eskimo boy. The sketching was done with a black crayon.

Balsa wood is so soft that you actually can sink your fingernails into it. You don't have to use a mallet when carving with the wood gouge. Just push the wood gouge as in Fig. 346.

You can forget about the wood gouge and do all the roughing out that is necessary with the wood rasp (Fig. 347).

Balsa wood is not a good wood for carving. Not only is it too soft, but it is very stringy or fibrous. It is almost impossible to get as clean a cut with the hand tools as you can if you are using mahogany or teak. As a matter of fact, it is not too different from trying to carve a ball of cotton or wool. The power tools carve this wood as if it were soft butter. Here in Fig. 348, the hair is being grooved in with a small, high-speed rotary file. This is absolutely no wood to use if you wish to try to carve

in details. Keep the carving simple. Furthermore, there is another reason for keeping your carving as simple as possible. *The melted lacquer is difficult to control.* You cannot do detailed inlay work with this medium, so there is no point in carving in a lot of detail in the first place.

Notice how in Fig. 349 the eyes, mouth, and nose are suggested only vaguely. There is no point in trying to work in any more detail than what you see in the illustration. Remember, this is not a carving in itself; it is only an armature on which the lacquer is to be applied. Do not let the prospect of carving the human head frighten you. It is no more difficult to carve than anything else, providing you do not strive for too much realism. If your carving suggests a face as well as this carving, it will be adequate.

Except for the grooving of the hair, all other carving on the face could have been done with the small sanding drum in Fig. 350. In fact, it is easier and better to shape this wood with abrasives than with the rotary files.

The lacquer either can be melted directly above the grooves and allowed to drip or run into them, or, as in Fig. 351, it can be melted away from the carving and then quickly spread or smeared over the grooves. In this latter method, you must learn to work very quickly because the lacquer sets or hardens almost instantly. Hold the lacquer stick to the flame, and, as soon as you see it beginning to melt, apply it to the carving. Both methods were used in applying the color to this carving.

Where you are applying the color to a fairly large area, as in Fig. 352, there is no difficulty. Hold the lacquer stick and torch a few inches above the carving, and, as the lacquer melts and runs onto the carving, spread the substance around with the lacquer stick. The eyes, nose and mouth will now be grooved, and black

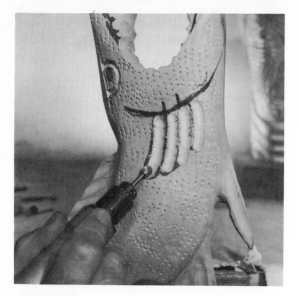

FIG. 340

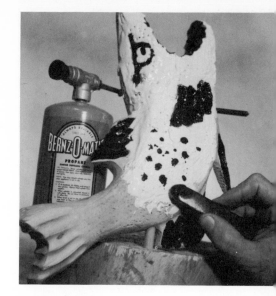

FIG. 341

FIG. 342

FIG. 343

FIG. 344

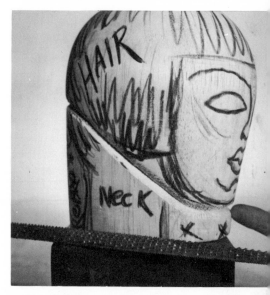

FIG. 345

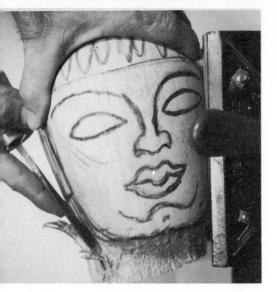

FIG. 346

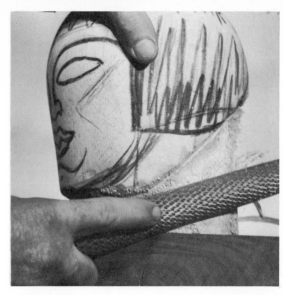

FIG. 347

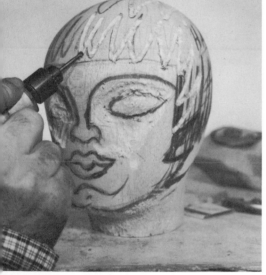

FIG. 348

FIG. 349

FIG. 350

FIG. 351

FIG. 352

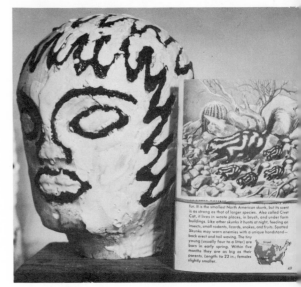

FIG. 353

lacquer will be melted over the grooves and allowed to fill them. Needless to say, this calls for a steady hand.

The carving in Fig. 353 is unfinished, but it is complete enough to give you an idea of what the finished carving would look like. Set a carving like this in a room so it is some distance from the viewer, and many would confuse it, even as crude as it is, with a piece of ceramic sculpture. But if you are just getting started with lacquering, do not begin with the human head; instead, start either with the fish carving or with one of the small skunks in the pocket book. These little skunks are really an ideal subject for this process. Since the color of a skunk is black and white, you can use shellac sticks which can be purchased almost anywhere. In shaping the wood to resemble a skunk, do not attempt to be too fussy—remember, the color of the lacquer is supposed to contribute something to the carving.

Inlaying with Plastic Wood

Fish Cross Sections

Saw a 1-inch disc off the end of a log of soft wood as in Fig. 354. Since you are going to inlay it, the grain of the wood isn't important. The cross section is being sawed off the end of a cypress knee. Notice how it already resembles a fish. The wood between the tail and fins and in the mouth can be sawed out or removed with a wood auger in the power drill.

Figure 355. As this is only an exercise, don't bother to round the body of the fish. Just shape the outline with the rasp so that it resembles a fish, and then sand lightly to make sketching easy. Sketch in any design that you please. Glance through the pocket book on fishes for ideas. You can make this sketch as involved or as simple as you choose. It will not affect the carving because you are carving into the grain of the wood to start with.

Trace over the design with a medium cutting burr in the hand grinder (Fig. 356). Make these grooves slightly less than ⅛ inch deep.

Spread the Plastic Wood over the grooves with a pallet knife as shown in Fig. 357. Plastic Wood dries quickly, so for each application cover an area no larger than about half the size of your hand. Be sure to close the can immediately, so that the Plastic Wood will not dry out.

Rub your thumbs lightly over some paste wax and press the Plastic Wood down hard into the grooves. Figure 358 is not the same carving as in Fig. 356, but the procedure is the same no matter what you are inlaying. As you can see in the illustration, the Plastic Wood shrinks slightly in drying. Do not worry. The carving will be leveled off while the surplus Plastic Wood is being removed with the sanding disc in the power tool.

After sanding off the surplus Plastic Wood, wax lightly and polish with the bonnet—lower right in Fig. 359. Both of these carvings are inlaid with only one color of Plastic Wood—the top one with walnut and the lower with gumwood. Other colors available are light and dark mahogany, cedar, oak, white, and, of course, natural. Neither one of these carvings is interesting, but they would have been improved somewhat had different colors of Plastic Wood been used. For example, you might try inlaying the tail, fins, eyes, and body of your carving each with a different-colored Plastic Wood. How to make your own colors with pure lacquer and using the natural Plastic Wood for a base is explained in this chapter in the section, "Coloring Plastic Wood." Liquid aluminum is an excellent material for inlay work. Follow the same procedure in Fig. 360 as was given for inlaying with the Plastic Wood.

Fish in the Round

The angry carp in Fig. 361 is 21 inches long. The fish, because its form can be

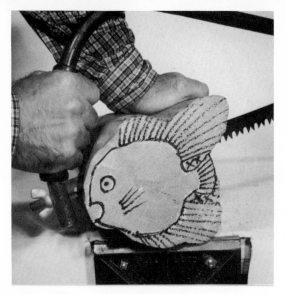

Fig. 354

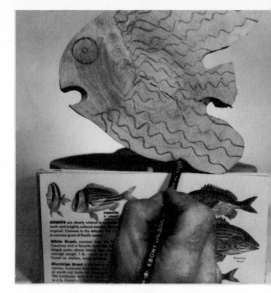

Fig. 355

Fig. 356

Fig. 357

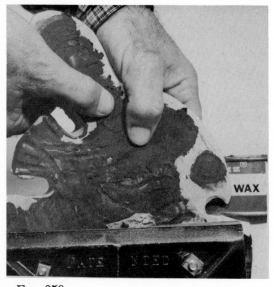

Fig. 358

Fig. 359

150

simplified, is by all odds the easiest way to make a start at inlaying. All that is required to arrive at the stage in the illustration is a soft board 1 inch thick by 2 or 3 inches wide, and a foot or so in length. The grain of the wood isn't too important in an inlay, so use the softest wood available. A small branch or trunk of a tree could be used just as well as a board. But for a first attempt, a section of soft board is perhaps best. Sketch a fish design on the board, using a picture of a fish as a guide for yourself.

After you've sketched in the outline of the fish on the board, rough it out with a saw, round the edges with a rasp, and sand the wood smooth enough so that it is easy to sketch on the surface with a soft lead pencil as on the fish depicted. For sanding, use the ¼-inch drill with a rubber backing pad to which you attach a medium sanding disc. (See Fig. 363 and the description on how to remove surplus Plastic Wood. The same suggestions apply to sanding in general.) In rasping or sanding the fish form, always remember that a fish—any fish—comes to a gradual point both at the head and tail and at the top and bottom. Don't worry about details at this stage. In inlay work, they aren't important. Anyway, the object is to make the inlay give the impression of a fish just as much as the form or shape of your carving.

For example, although a carp was used as a guide for the fish in the illustration, the fins are all wrong, and, although carp have teeth, they are not like the teeth sketched. Nor do carp have eyes as shown. Yet, the fish is unmistakably just what it is supposed to be—an angry fish. Don't worry about sanding it too smooth either; you're going to groove it in order to put in the inlay. Finally, keep the over-all design as simple as possible. Of course, you don't have to use the shape of the fish in this illustration as a guide nor

should you copy the sketching. Try out your own ideas.

Figure 362 demonstrates how to groove the fish for inlaying. A hand grinder is absolutely essential at this point. The smaller one pictured is more than adequate. It is much easier to handle and control than the larger one, yet is capable of doing the work required. Use the type of cutting burr that is in the larger hand grinder, and also a smaller-type version of the same cutting burr for more detailed work. Follow your sketch with the grinder the same as if you were retracing it with a pencil. Make the grooves about ⅛ inch deep and trace them about the same distance.

In this illustration, note how the grooving departs from the original sketch in Fig. 361. Instead of trying to imitate scales, which would have meant grooving against the grain of the wood, wavy lines have been grooved in instead. Not only was this much easier because you are grooving with the grain of the wood, but the wavy lines tend to convey the impression of movement. Notice, too, how the grooves in the fin bend backward. This also helps create the impression of a fish gliding through water. Compare Figs. 361 and 362 and you will notice that the latter is definitely an improvement, yet not nearly so difficult to make. The exposed teeth, and the straight line over the eyes are, of course, what make the fish look angry. The cutting burr described above leaves a rough, fuzzy edge on the grooves. Don't try to eliminate this. It helps to hold the Plastic Wood in the grooves.

In Fig. 363 we inlay the fish. For a beginning use only two colors, so that the work doesn't get too involved. Only walnut Plastic Wood was used on the fish. Study the illustration carefully; it tells you all you have to know about inlay work. To start the inlay, use the type of pallet knife shown. Dig the Plastic Wood out of

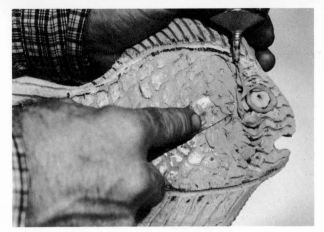

FIG. 360

FIG. 361

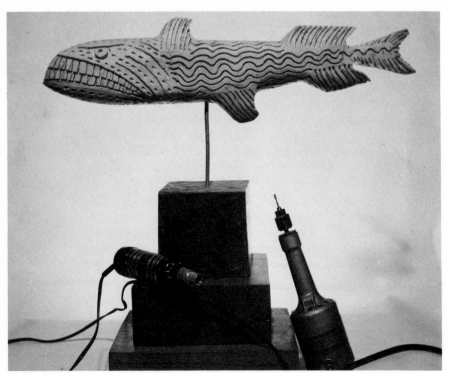

FIG. 362

152

FIG. 363

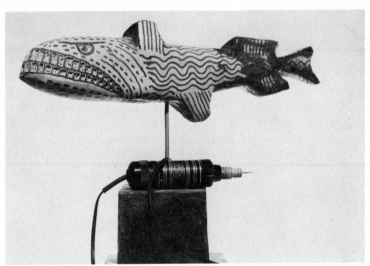

FIG. 364

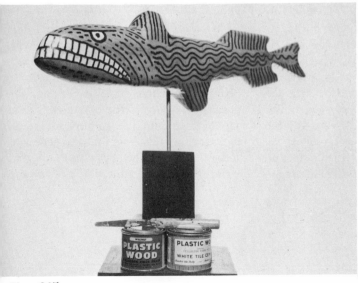

FIG. 365

the can and press it into the grooves of the wood. Learn to work fast, because Plastic Wood dries quickly. Press down hard on the pallet knife and don't worry about how messy the carving gets from the Plastic Wood bulging over the grooves—the surplus will be sanded off later.

Inlay only a small section at a time. Begin with the tail. Then close the can securely. Now, rub your thumb across some paste wax and press the Plastic Wood down hard into the grooves. Use only enough wax on your thumb to prevent the Plastic Wood from sticking. If the Plastic Wood is pressed down below the edges of the grooves, don't worry about it. It will all be evened up in the sanding process. Furthermore, as the Plastic Wood dries, it will shrink somewhat anyway. Unless the shrinkage is very pronounced, ignore it because the sanding process will take care of it. However, where it is very apparent that there is not enough Plastic Wood in the groove, then simply add some more. This is the reason you should not use too much wax on your thumb; Plastic Wood does not adhere to wax, and, if you have used too much, the added Plastic Wood will not take hold.

Now, repeat the same process, covering only the fin section, and so on, until the entire fish is inlaid. Allow the carving to dry a few hours or overnight, depending on the heat. Then, with the ¼-inch drill and sanding pad and disc pictured, sand off the surplus Plastic Wood around the eyes and mouth. This will only take a few minutes. Do not bother to sand the entire fish at this stage and do not use a sandpaper disc that is too coarse—a medium disc will do. If a sanding disc is too coarse it tends to tear the Plastic Wood back out of the grooves. The same thing will happen if you put too much pressure on the power tool.

Figure 364, grinding in the teeth and the eyes, really explains itself, except no-

tice how a tiny edge of wood has been left to protect the inlaid Plastic Wood outlining the teeth and the eyes. All this may look and sound involved, but it is very simple because the hand grinder and cutting burr do the work. You merely guide the grinder. Use a small cutting burr in the grinder. Now, fill in the teeth and the whites of the eyes with white Plastic Wood, and, while this is drying or setting, go over the rest of the fish with the sanding disc. Wherever you cannot reach with the large disc, use the smaller ones shown in Fig. 363. And wherever you cannot reach with these, as around the fins and tail, use the abrasive bands and rolls also shown. These rolls and bands are fastened to an abrasive arbor, which in turn is inserted in the ¼-inch drill. This enables you to sand almost anywhere. By this time, the white Plastic Wood in the teeth and eyes perhaps has dried enough so you can sand off the surplus which will allow the previous walnut inlay to show.

For the finished fish in Fig. 365, about 2½ cans of walnut Plastic Wood (each ¼ pound) and ⅓ of a can of white Plastic Wood were used. After you've sanded over the fish with the ¼-inch drill and medium sanding disc, go over it again with a 7/0 or an 8/0 garnet paper disc. Now give the carving a heavy coat of clear Firzite mixed 50-50 with benzine. This soaks right into the wood and seals it or primes it without giving it a cheap gloss. It also dries quickly—especially in the sun. When the fish is dry, go over it again with a 7/0 or an 8/0 garnet paper, but this time by hand. Then wax and polish with the bonnet until a high polish is achieved. Plastic Wood takes a high wax finish.

Now, find where the fish carving balances on your finger, drill a ¼-inch hole at that spot up into the carving about an inch. Drill another hole into the center of the base, insert a dowel pin and mount as in the illustration. However, do not use the bases in these illustrations as a guide. Their principal function was to block out the back floodlight in taking the pictures. Use your own judgment in selecting a base, or turn to Chapter 12, "Bases," for suggestions.

Note: It is best to drill the hole which will be used to mount the carving during the roughing-out stage. If you wait until the carving is entirely finished, you could damage it while clamping it in the vise in order to drill the hole. In any event, there is no point in waiting until the last minute to drill this hole.

Bird Form

The carving in Fig. 366 is 24 inches high and is inlaid with the four following colors: walnut, gumwood, and light and dark mahogany. The base is teakwood, and the author's name is inlaid with oak Plastic Wood.

To inlay different colors next to each other and close together, do this: groove the carving for one color at a time; inlay that groove; allow it to dry for several hours or overnight; sand off the surplus; and then, and only then, groove for the next color. If you did all the grooving at once, the colors would overlap in the inlaying process. For example, in this bird form the simulated feathers on the breast were grooved and then inlaid with light mahogany Plastic Wood. After drying, the surplus was sanded off, and the holes inside these simulated feathers were then carved and inlaid with gumwood. After this had dried, the surplus gumwood was sanded off. The back of the bird form was done in the same way, except that here the holes are inlaid with walnut.

This carving, by the way, is hollow and looks best if viewed below eye level. A low bookcase or coffee table seems to be about the right place for it. The base for the carving appears correct. The carving was fastened to the base with three or four wooden dowel pins which had first been coated with a glue or cement. If you are using a thin base such as this, a better way to mount a carving on it is with wood screws which you twist up into the carving from the bottom of the base. Naturally, these wood screws are countersunk into the bottom of the base. Detailed illustrated instructions on how this is done are in Chapter 12, "Bases." Finally, this carving was given a very thorough waxing, which means six or eight coats, with polishing between each coat.

Old Penguin

Walnut and light and dark mahogany Plastic Wood were used in the inlay in Fig. 367. A carving this size (29 inches) takes between eight and a dozen 1/4-pound cans. This carving will stand very well by itself and needs no base. A cypress knee was used that in its natural state already clearly suggested this carving. The only wood that had to be removed was the wood below the breast of the bird, and, of course, the wings had to be carved. As you can see, this is a very easy carving to make. Use a section of a small log and do the roughing out with the hatchet and wood rasp. Should the wood you are using have a pronounced grain, then by all means emphasize and bring out this grain and forget about the inlaying. Never, but never, allow detailed surface carving or inlaying interfere with the grain of the wood, especially if it is outstanding. A good policy is to use your own judgment and common sense. Should you come across a piece of wood with a very interesting or beautiful grain, the chances are that the *less you carve or interfere* with this grain, the better your carving will be. Let the grain of the wood do the work.

What this means in terms of the penguin carving in the illustration is that all you would have to do is suggest the wings of the bird and, of course, its general outline. You would not even have to carve in the eyes and bill. The point to be stressed here is that a piece of wood with a rich grain and color is a beautiful thing in itself and, as such, the less you do to it the better. Unfortunately, pieces of such wood, suitable for a carving in the round, are not common and, when found, are fairly expensive. They are frankly too expensive for the beginner or the experimenter. And only a very few lumber companies or artist supply houses stock such hardwood logs for carving purposes. Until you have gained some experience at carving, perhaps it is best to forget about these exotic imported hardwood logs, and instead concentrate on whatever local wood is available.

Coloring Plastic Wood— Weather Vane

The weather vane in Fig. 368 is 3 feet tall and is inlaid with natural Plastic Wood, colored with pure lacquer. The colors are blue, green, red, yellow, black, and orange. A good way to color Plastic Wood is with automobile lacquer. This is not the automobile lacquer available in supply stores, but rather the pure concentrated lacquer from which automobile lacquer is made. About two or three tablespoons of this lacquer will color a $\frac{1}{4}$-pound can of Plastic Wood, and color it to a bright red, blue, or whatever color of lacquer you are using. All you do is stir it in the natural Plastic Wood. It blends very easily. Not only does this lacquer color the Plastic Wood to any desired shade, but it even appears to increase the adhesive qualities of Plastic Wood and as such increases its permanency. The inlay in this illustration, for example, was done several years ago, and, although subject to various temperature changes and other conditions, is the same today as when the carving was inlaid. In the entire 3-foot carving, there is not a single instance where the inlay has shrunk, pulled away from the wood, cracked, or come loose. And just as important, the addition of this concentrated lacquer does not in any way make the Plastic Wood any more difficult to handle. Of course, there must be many other ways of coloring Plastic Wood. If this material interests you, one way of finding out is to experiment. Whatever type of color you add to the Plastic Wood, it must not lessen its adhesive qualities.

The single tail feather in this carving was carved in and is not stuck there. It is part of the wood. It is slightly curved and is not much more than $\frac{1}{4}$ inch thick at its widest. Even though carved with the grain of the wood, it would immediately snap off if the carving were dropped. This sort of thing is plainly not worth the effort involved. In fact, the carving might look better if the tail feather were not there at all. The colors of this tail feather are red, blue, green, black, and yellow. The bands of color are less than $\frac{1}{8}$ inch apart. To repeat, in inlaying different colors this close together, you groove and inlay each color separately. Using the feather in the bird form in Fig. 368 as an illustration, first make all the grooves in the feather that are going to be inlaid in red. After inlaying the red color, groove next to it for the blue or whatever color you are using. In other words, if you were to inlay six different colors next to each other—about $\frac{1}{8}$ inch apart—and if you made all the grooves at once, it would be difficult when applying the colors to keep them from overlapping. Whereas, if you groove for each color separately, you don't have to worry about the color overlapping into the next groove.

Figure 369 is a tropical bird form carved from driftwood. Since the driftwood suggested the form of the bird, very little carving was necessary. The sweep of the tail and the body of the bird were already

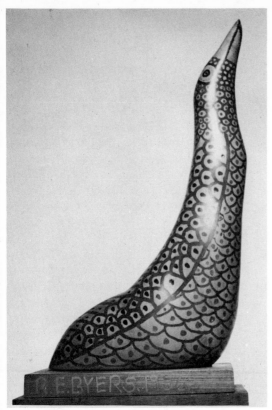

FIG. 366

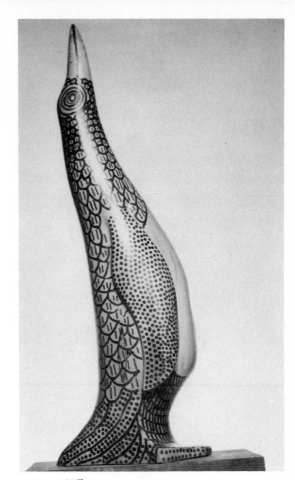

FIG. 367

FIG. 368

FIG. 369

FIG. 370

FIG. 371

there, and only the head and neck had to be roughed out and shaped.

Figure 370 shows in detail the real work involved in Fig. 369. When it is realized that this carving is 3 feet long; that every inch or half an inch of the surface of the wood is inlaid; that at least eight or ten different colors were used; and, finally, that each one of these colors had to be inlaid separately; then some idea can be gained of the patience required to complete the job. If there were any rhyme or reason to the design of the inlay and the arrangement of the colors, there might be some justification for all this work. As it is, it is a good example of what not to do. Before attempting something similar, it might be best to visit your local public library and at least glance through a book or two on design.

Figure 371 is entitled Worried Woman and is the detail of a carving made from a 4-foot section of a cypress root. It is inlaid with Plastic Wood colored with lacquer.

Bases

The bases in Fig. 372 are from the bottom up: three blocks of African mahogany, two of Indian teak, and three each of walnut and cypress. Three bases are inlaid with color. One—top left—with green-colored Plastic Wood, and the other two with melted lacquer. The name and date on the bases were carved in with the small hand grinder with a medium cutting burr. Some are inlaid with different-colored Plastic Wood, some with metal. Naturally, if you were exhibiting your work, this name would appear on the back and not the front of the base.

All bases in Fig. 373 are lignum vitae. The largest piece is only 11 inches by 5 inches by 5 inches. The pieces on the top and the bottom marked with the O are 8 inches by 3 inches by 1½ inches. Yet this wood is so heavy that the combined weight of these few small pieces comes to more than 150 pounds. These blocks, because of the numerous checks in them, are unsuitable for carving. They will be sawed to different sizes and then sanded and polished for bases. Because of the weight and rich color and grain, they make excellent bases. They give your carving an expensive look. The pieces marked with an O are already polished on two sides and have a very subtle bevel. This bevel—a slight bulge—is so gradual as to be barely visible. It was made by machine, for it obviously would be very difficult—considering the extreme hardness of the

wood—to do anything like this by hand. These pieces are used to pack the bearings on a ship, which will give you an idea of the hardness of the wood. The O on the wood is perhaps the lumberman's code. Lignum vitae is, of course, one of the hardest and heaviest of woods.

What Base to Use—If Any

If your carving can stand alone, don't bother with a base. The only time to use one is when the carving cannot stand alone, or when a base definitely adds something to the carving. The base must become a part of the whole design. At no time allow the base to dominate the carving or to detract from it. A base too bulky, too thin, too tall, or too wide will do this. On the other hand, too small a base will not only weaken the appearance of the whole thing, but the carving actually may topple over.

A highly polished base definitely adds something to a rough, vigorous, direct carving. So does the reverse—a highly finished carving on a rough base. Study illustrations of sculpture for ideas. In general, a tricky, or odd-shaped base not only fails to add to the carving, but may detract from it. Always remember that the base is secondary to the carving. The only function of the base is to support the carving, so keep it conservative and inconspicuous. Whenever possible, the base should be made to appear as a continuation or a part of the carving. The best way to decide what base to use is to have many different-shaped bases in various stages of finish and in various woods so that you can experiment with them in order to determine the one best suited for the carving in question.

Finally, remember that many times your carving will look best if hung on a wall.

A fish carving, unlike any other (animal or bird), cannot stand alone. Unless it is to be hung on a wall, it will need a base. Carvings of fish, both in stone and wood, have been mounted very effectively on broken pieces of marble, chunks of glass, and even field stones. This not only involves a lot of work but requires special tools, so for a beginning only wooden bases will be considered.

If you are using a hardwood for a base, such as mahogany, walnut, teak, etc., you might as well emphasize it by polishing and waxing it. Drill a hole in the center of the wood and mount the fish carving (presumably a hole already has been drilled into the carving). Whenever possible, fit the carving flush to the base; that is, do not have the dowel pin showing. Where it is not going to be seen, a wooden dowel pin will do. But often the fish will be so carved that a portion of the dowel will show where it joins the carving to the base. In this case, use a metal dowel pin—brass or bronze.

You don't have to use expensive hardwoods for bases. Often a base made out of a piece of cheap rough pine will show off a highly finished carving in a very interesting manner. Especially is this true if the pine base is weather-beaten or bleached by the sun. Two or three inches sawed off the end of a small- or medium-sized fence post that has been exposed to the weather for years makes an excellent base for a fairly large carving of a fish. Sometimes a rough block of cheap pine painted with a dull black paint or enamel

sets off a highly finished carving just right. In painting a base, it is best to use black, and always a dull or flat black. In staining a base, use a deep brown.

Don't worry too much about bases. The main rule to remember is to work out some sort of balance between the carving and the base. If the carving looks right on the base, the chances are that it is the right one. Incidentally, for some reason or other, you more often will err on the side of using a base that is too large instead of one that is too small. Watch this tendency, because a base that is too large dwarfs the carving. Although it is generally best to avoid using tricky or cute or clever bases, some fish carvings could be mounted on a piece of driftwood. Try it, but keep in mind that you are exhibiting a fish carving and not a piece of driftwood to which a fish carving has been attached.

There is no problem to drilling the hole in most bases. Simply find the center of the base and drill a hole there. Naturally, this hole must correspond to the one already drilled into the fish. A good policy, if your carving is not too small, is to drill the same size hole in all your carvings. In all but a very few of the carvings in these pictures, the hole is $\frac{1}{4}$ inch round and about 1 inch deep. This means that you can buy a $\frac{1}{4}$-inch dowel pin, knowing that it will fit all your carvings.

There will be times when drilling a hole in the exact center of the base will throw the carving off balance. In this case, ignore the center of the base and drill the hole in the base so the carving will be balanced. Should you make a mistake in drilling the hole in either the base or the carving, don't worry about it. Plug up the hole and try again.

Drill the hole in a fish carving at the center of balance. In nine out of ten times this will be the correct place, and remember to do this before the carving is brought to a point. This is particularly important if the wood you are using is thin.

Everything is wrong in Fig. 374. A simple carving like this does not warrant all this base. It is much too tall and too involved. Avoid using a base where the base on which you are mounting your carving in turn needs a base.

In general, a long thin base with the carving fitted flush to it seems just about the right arrangement for a fish carving as shown in Fig. 375. The carving is African mahogany, and the base is lignum vitae, also from Africa. It is the natural beauty of these two pieces of wood that makes this a fair carving and not necessarily the carving itself.

If you have several fish carvings around, try mounting them in groups either on a base or on the wall. For a base, use a cross section of a small tree (Fig. 376). Small eye hooks can be used to hang the carvings on the wall (Fig. 377).

Should you drill the hole in your fish carving off center as in Fig. 378, then at least stain the dowel pin so it will not be so noticeable. This sort of thing makes a carving look amateurish.

It is inevitable that at some time or other you will drill the hole in your carving at the wrong angle, and, because of this, the carving will not set right on the base. Instead of drilling another hole, do what you see in Fig. 379. Instead of using a wooden dowel pin (as on the right), which of course cannot be bent, use a metal one, and bend it until the carving does set right on the base. This one is ¼-inch aluminum wire which bends very easily.

A bird carving such as the eagle in Fig. 380 is difficult to mount. The legs are wood, wrapped with wire, and then coated with aluminum. Had the legs been eliminated, then a single hole drilled into the breast, and the carving mounted flush to the base, the piece might have been more

attractive and would have involved a lot less work.

The unfinished horse in Fig. 381 is another difficult carving for which to figure out a base. It is 2 feet thick at the neck, and thus would require at least a 2½-foot-square base. For proper balance, this base should be at least 6 inches thick. A chunk of wood that size easily could cost more than the carving is worth. Anyway, the carving will stand alone, so forget about a base.

The base of Indian teak in Fig. 382 seems just exactly right for this carving.

Figure 383 is a school of angry fish about 6 feet in height. The base is a large cross section of a tree into which many holes have been drilled. You can rearrange a group like this merely by shifting the carvings from one dowel pin to another. Since the holes in all the carvings are identical, this is no problem.

Figure 384 is the opposite view of the school of angry fish. Notice how the bottom four fish are carved differently on each side.

Figure 385 is a school of fish made up of a group of wood discs.

Mounting the Carving on the Base

1

To mount a carving on a base into which a hole has already been drilled, the problem is to decide where to drill the hole into the bottom of the carving so that it will correspond to the one already drilled into the base.

First, place your carving in its exact position on the base and draw a chalk line around the piece for a future guide.

Figure 386. Now twist a piece of chalk around in the hole in the base until a fine mound of chalk dust forms around the edges of the hole.

Figure 387. Replace the carving on the base, using the chalk line that you previously drew as a guide.

Fig. 372

Fig. 373

FIG. 374

FIG. 375

FIG. 376

FIG. 377

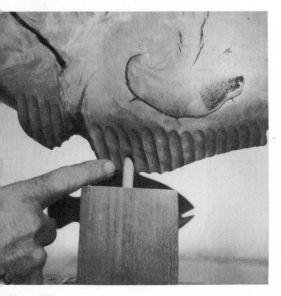

FIG. 378

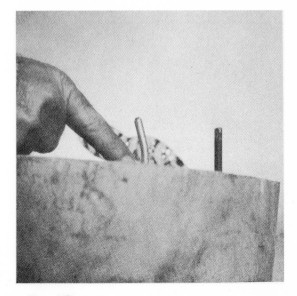

FIG. 379

F‍IG. 380

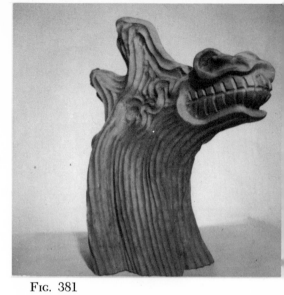

F‍IG. 381

F‍IG. 382

F‍IG. 383

Fig. 384

Fig. 385

Fig. 386

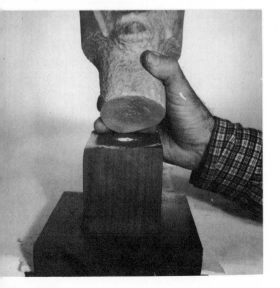

Fig. 387

Fig. 388

165

Figure 388. Press the carving down hard.

Figure 389. Lift up the carving. Enough of the chalk dust will adhere to the bottom of the carving to form a faint circle. Drill the hole into the center of this circle.

Note: Here, as in the illustrations that follow, the chalk was exaggerated deliberately in order to insure getting a picture that would illustrate the procedure clearly.

2

A still easier way to mount your carving is to use wood screws, especially where the base is not too thick.

Figure 390. Place the carving where it belongs and trace around it with a piece of chalk. The X on the base is to remind you that this is the front of the base.

Figure 391. Now lift up the carving and make two small X's where you are going to drill two very small holes. Keep these X's well away from the edges of the chalk circle.

Figure 392. With a small drill, drill down through the base.

Figure 393. Turn the base over and countersink the two small holes. You can use the high-speed rotary file in the hand grinder to do this. Now insert the two wood screws so that they protrude from the top of the base about a quarter inch or so.

Figure 394. Press down the carving on the protruding screws, using the chalk line as a guide. In this illustration, the tips of the screws are barely visible.

Figure 395. Press the carving down real hard, forcing the screws to dent the bottom of the carving.

Figure 396. Raise the carving and notice where the screws dented the bottom of it. Drill up into the carving about an inch at these dents, using the same small drill you used to drill down through the base. The point of all this is to give the wood screws a chance to get started into the base. This is especially important if your carving is made of very hard wood.

Figure 397. Fit the carving back on the base and tighten the screws.

Figure 398. Finished. Actually, this base should be a little thicker and a little larger. As it is, you get the impression that it might topple over.

3

If your carving is small and light, it is not necessary to anchor it to the base very firmly. Although people might like to handle the carving, they surely aren't going to try to pry it loose from the base. Therefore, in this instance, a good contact cement ought to do. Make certain that the carving is properly centered on the base.

If your carving is large and you are using a large base, the best way to fasten it is with a dowel pin or a metal tube. Place the carving in the correct position on the base. Then trace around it with a pencil. Remove the carving and find the exact center of both the bottom of the carving and the center of the pencil sketch on the top of the base. Using a $\frac{1}{4}$-inch or $\frac{3}{8}$-inch drill, drill holes about an inch or so in the center of both the base and the bottom of the carving. Then insert the dowel pin in the base and anchor the carving. If this still doesn't appear strong enough, apply some contact cement to the dowel pin before you connect the carving to the base.

Where the dowel pin or metal tube will show, the proper centering of it in both the carving and in the base is important, or it will throw the carving off balance— or at least give it the appearance of being off balance. But, where the carving fits flush to the base, this isn't important; so here is a simpler method.

Figure 399. Place your carving on the base in the exact position you want it to be. The carving should look well balanced

FIG. 389

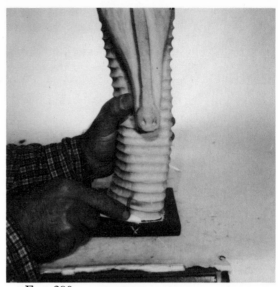

FIG. 390

FIG. 391

FIG. 392

FIG. 393

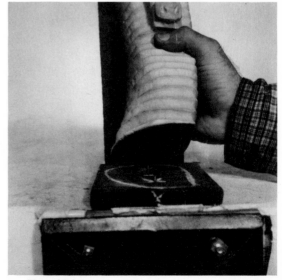

FIG. 394

167

on the base. This does not always mean placing the carving in the exact center of the base. Now trace around the bottom of the carving with a sharpened piece of chalk.

Figure 400. Next, without shifting the carving either to the right or the left or backward or forward, carefully lift a corner of the carving up and slip a piece of chalk under it about in the center of the chalk line.

Figure 401. Press the carving down hard, using the chalk line on the base to make certain the carving is in its exact position on the base.

Figure 402. Now lift up the carving. Enough chalk will adhere to the bottom of the carving to act as a guide for drilling. With a ⅜-inch wood auger in the ¼-inch drill, drill a hole 1 inch deep into both the bottom of the carving and into the top of the base, using the chalk marks as a guide. Insert a 2-inch dowel pin (wooden and naturally ⅜ inch around) into the base and remount the carving. To make the mounting more permanent, place some contact cement around both ends of the wooden dowel pin.

Note: When following this procedure, do not use as much chalk as is shown in the illustrations. The smaller the piece of chalk you slide under the carving, the more accurate the chalk guide will be. A tiny piece, the size of a pinhead is adequate. Also, when you lift your carving, not as much chalk will adhere to the bottom of it as in Fig. 402.

Leveling the Base of a Carving

To level the base of a carving, do the following:

Figure 403. Cover a surface that you know to be perfectly level with an even coat of black crayon. The surface shown is a ¼-inch slab of a broken glass table top.

Figure 404. Slide the base of your carv-ing in a circular motion over the crayon-covered surface.

Figure 405. The black spots are high spots in your carving.

Figure 406. Sand the high or black spots off and repeat the process until the base of the carving is level.

Figure 407. Leveling the bottom of a carving so that it will fit flush to the base can at times turn into a difficult and time-consuming job. One way of overcoming this problem is to sand down the center of the bottom of your carving about ⅛ inch or so, being careful not to sand down the outer edge of the base. At least now you won't have to worry about high spots in the center of the base. All you have to do is level the outer edge. Yet, no matter how hard you try, there will still be times when it virtually will be impossible to get the bottom of the carving to fit perfectly level on the base. When this happens, stop trying, for, after all, it could be that the base on which you are trying to fit the carving is uneven. If you get your carving on the bottom as level as the one in the illustration (note black spots around edge of base, but none in the center), that is close enough. For this base to be perfectly level, the outer edge should be all black.

Repairing the Rotten or Decayed Wood in a Carving

Regardless of what wood you are using, you will from time to time come across a decayed section. Generally speaking, this will be a knot in the wood. If these decayed sections were limited to the surface of the wood, you could, of course, avoid them by simply not using the wood. But they may turn up inside the wood after a great deal of carving already has been done. When this happens, don't abandon the carving; the wood can be fixed easily.

Figure 408. Dig out as much of the decayed part as is practical, and, while

Fɪɢ. 397

Fɪɢ. 398

Fɪɢ. 399

Fɪɢ. 400

F<small>IG</small>. 401

F<small>IG</small>. 402

F<small>IG</small>. 403

F<small>IG</small>. 404

F<small>IG</small>. 405

FIG. 406

FIG. 407

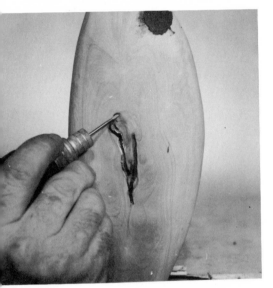

FIG. 408

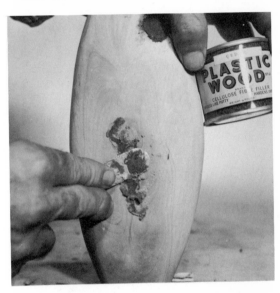

FIG. 409

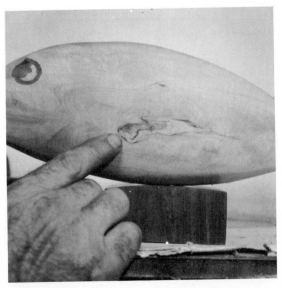

FIG. 410

you are doing so, undercut the good part of the wood. To do this, use a medium- or large-size cutting burr in the hand grinder. You undercut the good or firm part of the wood in order to give the filler you are going to use a chance to take hold.

Figure 409. Select a Plastic Wood—in this case cedar—that matches the carving and press it down hard into the groove or hole from which the decayed wood has been removed. (There are other products on the market besides Plastic Wood and they are undoubtedly just as good. One of them is Duratite and it comes in at least as many colors as Plastic Wood. The Duratite product comes in two grades, a filler and a wood dough. For the above, use the wood dough.

Figure 410. Once the Plastic Wood has dried, sand off the surplus. If you selected the proper color Plastic Wood, the repairs to the wood will not be too noticeable. If the hole in the wood you are repairing is fairly large and deep, then first drive a wooden wedge into it. Use the same wood as the carving is made of. Spread some contact cement both in the hole in the carving and on the wedge. Now finish sealing up the hole with a Plastic Wood that blends with the carving.

What to Avoid

The four angry fish carvings—two views of each—which comprise Figs. 411–418 have the following in common:

1. They are all large carvings.

2. Each fish was carved differently on each side.

3. Almost all the carving on these fishes is against the grain, which means, especially considering their size, that it would have been an almost impossible task to do this using hand tools.

4. All carving was done with hand grinders. The cutting accessories were the large-sized cutting burr and various-shaped, high-speed rotary files. Since the hand grinder does the actual work, no hard labor was involved, but in carvings this size, a certain amount of patience is required.

5. Very little if any previous sketching was done on the wood with a pencil or chalk. Instead, the design was worked out as the carving progressed. In other words, these are really freehand sketches, except that power tools and wood were substi-tuted for a sketching pad and a pencil.

Note that, because of the twist or curve in the body in three of the fishes, and especially because of the prominent teeth in all four, and again, because of their size, these fish carvings do have a crude vitality. Where would you exhibit them? Certainly not in the living room of a home. But they could be hung very effectively on the wall of a lakeside cottage or fishing camp, or perhaps even on the wall of a basement den or playroom.

I would suggest that you do not try to be cute or clever in your initial attempts. Undertake your first carvings with sincerity and you will be pleased to find that the finished work will usually reflect the honesty and the seriousness of your effort.

This does not mean that you should rule out the light-hearted, the gay, or even the humorous, but you will find that you can succeed far better with caricature or burlesque after you have developed some proficiency with serious or realistic objects.

FIG. 411

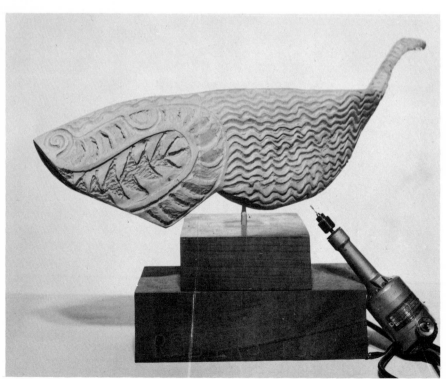

FIG. 412

174

FIG. 413

FIG. 414

FIG. 415

FIG. 416

Fig. 417

Fig. 418

Index